# TOMORROW NEVER KNOWS

## THIRTY YEARS OF BEATLES MUSIC
## AND MEMORABILIA

"I declare that the Beatles are Divine Messiahs. The wisest, holiest, most effective Avatars that the human race has yet produced. My thesis is a simple one.  It is my contention that John Lennon, George Harrison, Paul McCartney and Ringo Starr are mutants, prototypes of a new young race of laughing Freemen. Evolutionary agents sent by God, endowed with the mysterious power to create a new human species . . ."

Timothy Leary, 1967


"This is only the beginning, this sixties bit was just waking up in the morning and we haven't even gotten to dinner time yet. I can't wait, I'm so glad to be around. It's just going to be great and there's going to be more of us. So whatever you're thinking there, Mrs. Grundy of Sussex, Birmingham-on-Toast, you know you don't stand a chance. (A) You're not going to be there when we're running it, and (B), you'll like it when you get less frightened of it. So 'they' – whoever 'they' are – don't stand a chance, as they can't beat LOVE. Because all those old bits from religion about love being all powerful are true!"

John Lennon, 1969

# TOMORROW NEVER KNOWS

## THIRTY YEARS OF BEATLES MUSIC AND MEMORABILIA

### GEOFFREY GIULIANO

Paper Tiger

Paper Tiger
A Dragon's World Ltd Imprint
Limpsfield
Surrey RH8 0DY
Great Britain

First published by Dragon's World Ltd 1991

ISBN 1 85028 156 4

EDITORS  Michael Downey, James Adams
DESIGNERS  Eian Macmeeking, Cath Speight
ART DIRECTOR  Dave Allen
EDITORIAL DIRECTOR  Pippa Rubinstein


Typeset by Dragon's World Ltd / Pressdata, London
Printed in Portugal

Note: Neither the author or publishers of this book condone the
manufacture, distribution or sale of so-called bootleg recordings. The
bootlegging of material belonging to any group or individual is both strictly
illegal and reprehensible. The bootlegs in this book are included solely for
the purpose of historical accuracy.

# CONTENTS

The first part of the chapter titles are names of unreleased or obscure recordings made by the Beatles between 1963 and 1970.

*The Beatles, circa 1968.*

# PEACE OF MIND

## INTRODUCTION

It all seems like a dream now: four turned-on musical messiahs from the north of England sweeping up the youthful hopes of an entire generation on the magical crest of a wave still largely undiminished in force after three decades. The Beatles were, without question, the single greatest power in popular music we have seen. But beyond that the group helped suggest to so many the hidden creative potential buried deep within themselves.

For any work as broad and appealing as that accomplished by the Beatles, a little intensified investigation is justified. So much more so as the years roll along, with the measured, heavy thud of the showy and shallow nineties replacing the tribal drumbeat of the magical sixties. If the Beatles seemed the harbingers of a new, more enlightened era based on the user-friendly concepts of love, peace and the quest for enlightenment, then the current crop of potentate pop stars such as Madonna, Janet Jackson, M. C. Hammer and Whitney Houston sing in a far more cynical, decidedly less sincere age of personal prestige and materialism.

That's not to say that this second-generation music business is bad. It's just that it isn't nearly as fulfilling or seemingly necessary as

*The author at home.*

the ground-breaking territory covered by the Beatles and company. And it isn't nearly as much fun. Which is why so many of us who were there seem content to look longingly over our shoulders. It is the reason I think the Beatles are still important and should not be forgotten. It is the reason I put together this book.

Those who dedicate themselves to gathering up the remaining pieces of the artistic jigsaw left by the group do a service far beyond mere "souvenir collecting." Imagine if someone had been around to dog the likes of Beethoven, Einstein, Gandhi, Picasso or Hemingway in the same exacting, unedited way. Like veteran hippie A. J. Weberman plowing through Bob Dylan's garbage, searching for remnants of the great poet's loose change, these cultural detectives help preserve a side of our heroes that would otherwise remain unseen and forgotten. *The Beatles Album* seeks to contribute to the admirable chore of providing a visual document of the Beatles' great musical work. Inside you will find the very best of the Beatles' collective rarities. As an ensemble these valuable icons of the fabulous Beatle years tell a story much deeper than the meteoric rise to superstardom of John Lennon, Paul McCartney, George Harrison and Ringo Starr. "Remember man," Lennon once told me, "the Beatles really were just the music." So many years later this is all we have left — remarkably untarnished and every bit as vital as ever.

Although a couple of years back I discreetly sold off the bulk of my collection, piece by piece, to various clients throughout the world, I couldn't bear to sell any of my records. After more than 25 years of carefully selecting only the very best vinyl I could lay my hands on, I decided the love and care that had gone into it all was just too important to trade off for money. Today, as I look through my collection (and now this book), I see a whole hell of a lot more than a couple of hundred old records. Here is my youth: my crazy hippie/yippie days, my destitute college years, my early life as an actor on the dinner-theatre

circuit, my marriage and the birth of our four kids, the death of my parents and the sad passing of my elder brother Robert in 1990 from AIDS. In other words, my life. I suspect it's the same for many of you, too.

One wonders what life in our time might have been without the energetic presence of the Beatles. Still, as wonderful as they were, the Beatles as a phenomenon belong now chiefly to the past. But it is a friendly past that at least some of us today can still happily share. As for those who missed that first great thunder of Beatlemania, it is to you I dedicate this book. Here's hoping you're as touched and inspired by the Beatles' marvellous homemade melodies as we were.

Now that Beatlemania begins to move towards its fourth energetic decade, it is clear that the Beatles as an historical musical phenomenon will be with us for a long, long time, their great work garnering an ever deeper, more esteemed presence in our lives. Forget what you hear people say about artists owing a debt to the public. As far as the Fab Four are concerned, any such obligation was honoured long ago and has now turned itself squarely around. It is we who owe them.

Geoffrey Giuliano
Key West, Florida

# 1

## SHAKIN' IN THE SIXTIES

## BEATLE LPS

For most people, the Beatle LPs make up the bulk of what they consider to be the group's finest compositions. Highly accessible and undeniably entertaining, the Fabs' many high-powered albums – 13 were released in the UK during the group's existence, 19 in the US – neatly showcase their work as ultra-talented tunesmiths.

Equally involved in all phases of the production of their records, the Beatles showered great attention on the visuals of their album covers as well as on the revolutionary sounds contained within. Never before in the brief history of pop had what was on the *outside* of a record attained such importance to both the artists and their audience. The LP sleeve became more than just a functional way of packaging; it was now an artifact in its own right. From Robert Freeman's dramatic shadowy headshots for *Meet The Beatles* and the lacey extravagance of Beatle confidant Klaus Voorman's classic illustration for *Revolver,* to the psychedelic power of *Sgt. Pepper* and *Magical Mystery Tour*, the Beatles continually challenged their fans to expand their own concepts of what an album should look like and what a rock band should be.

*The Fab Four as we all remember them.*

Sometimes, however, fans and critics read things into the Beatles' record jackets that simply were not there. The most ridiculous misinterpretation of the group's graphics occurred in October 1969, when Russ Gibbs, a Detroit disc jockey at station WKNR, reported that, according to a series of "clues" hidden on various Beatle albums, Paul McCartney had been killed in a fiery car crash in 1966. In addition, rumour had it that a young McCartney look-a-like by the name of William Campbell had secretly taken over for the fallen Beatle at the request of the other three. Soon frantic fans everywhere were studying all the Beatles' covers for further clues. Eventually, two intrepid reporters from America's *Life* magazine made the trek to McCartney's rural hideaway near Campbeltown, Scotland and confronted the bemused Beatle who quite aptly commented: "If I were dead I'd be the last to know."

Never impressed with the never-ending waves of media tripe hawking the so-called deep "inner significance" of their latest album cover art, the boys fought back graphically in 1968 by commissioning artist John Kosh to design a stark, all-white pictureless sleeve to accompany the thirty-song opus entitled simply *The Beatles*. Twenty years later, George Harrison recalled other even more unusual plans for the now classic double album. "It was originally intended to have a clear see-through sleeve with a see-through record inside.

"When the record company said they couldn't do that we decided to have a white record with a white sleeve, but they wouldn't even do that. Yet they'd had red see-throughs when we were in Hamburg in 1960! Anyway, a couple of years later everybody had psychedelic picture discs . . . . I can't understand how we could have been so weak-willed. We also had Gandhi on the original artwork for *Sgt. Pepper* but the record company said, 'Sorry but you can't have him on there.' When we asked why not, they said, 'Because *some people* respect him.'"

Despite the trials of being light years ahead of their time, the Beatles managed to create several other eye-catching album jackets, including the stylized ceremonial crossing at Abbey Road and the lavish British boxed-set version of their eclectic swan song *Let It Be*. Over the years, various Beatle-related compilation albums have been released by EMI and its American counterpart, Capitol, but graphically none of them approached the high standard of creativity and design demanded by the Beatles during their tumultuous time together.

Here for your inspection is a selection of the finest examples of collectable Beatle LPs from the last 30 years of our on-going love affair with the Fabs. Included are several obscure foreign pressings and a wide range of early nonsense from the "anything goes" days of Beatlemania in America. On a more exalted level, here are also the real gems: the original album sleeves produced under the creative direction of the Beatles themselves.

*A limited-edition insert included in the Japanese version of* THE BEATLES/1967–1970.

*A 1984 POP (point of purchase) promo poster marking two decades of incomparable music from the world's greatest group, 1964 to 1984.*

NEW PARLOPHONE SINGLE R5620

ALL YOU NEED IS LOVE
THE·BEATLES

C/W BABY YOU'RE A RICH MAN

E.M.I. Records (The Gramophone Co. Ltd.) E.M.I. House, 20 Manchester Sq. London W.1

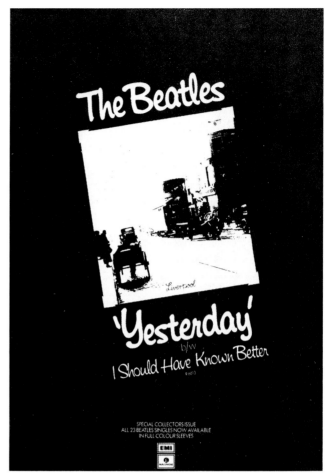

The Beatles

'Yesterday'
b/w
I Should Have Known Better

SPECIAL COLLECTORS ISSUE
ALL 23 BEATLES SINGLES NOW AVAILABLE
IN FULL COLOUR SLEEVES

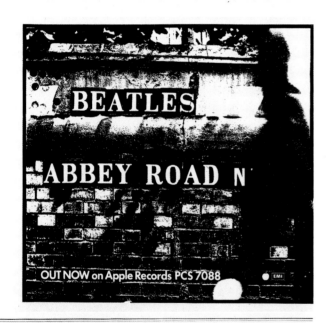

BEATLES
ABBEY ROAD N

OUT NOW on Apple Records PCS 7088

The Beatles!

NEW LP!    NEW EP!    NEW SINGLE!

We can work it out c/w Day Tripper

Parlophone PCS3075 PMC1267    Parlophone GEP8946

'PENNY LANE'    'STRAWBERRY FIELDS FOREVER'    THE BEATLES

PARLOPHONE OUT FRIDAY FEBRUARY 17 1967

*Original newspaper ads promoting the latest Beatle releases.*

*The Dutch version of the Beatles' LOVE SONGS. This striking stylized portrait of the Beatles by famed artist Patrick was originally intended as the cover illustration for what would later become known as the "WHITE ALBUM" (Parlophone Records, date unknown).*

*The first great wave of Beatlemania in the USA:* **TOP ROW** AIN'T SHE SWEET, *an Atco Records release of the Hamburg-era Beatles and the Swallows, as well as an assortment of tunes from other lesser known groups of the day (1964);* INTRODUCING THE BEATLES, *the Vee Jay label original of the group's British best seller (1963);* **SECOND ROW** *An awkward mishmash of music and interviews in* SONGS, PICTURES AND STORIES OF THE FABULOUS BEATLES, *also from the Vee Jay people (1964); New York producer Bob Gallo's Savage Records dynamic duo* THIS IS THE SAVAGE YOUNG BEATLES *and* **(BOTTOM)** *the feeble Pete Best solo fiasco* BEST OF THE BEATLES *(1966).*

*The seldom appreciated back covers to:* **TOP ROW** THE BEATLES' SECOND ALBUM
*(Capitol Records, 1964);* REVOLVER *(Capitol Records, 1966);* **SECOND ROW** A HARD DAY'S NIGHT
*(Capitol Records, 1964);* BEATLES VI *(Capitol Records, 1965);* **BOTTOM ROW** *The trendsetting*
RUBBER SOUL *(Capitol Records, 1965).*

LEFT COLUMN, ABOVE *A mid-eighties promotional poster celebrating the impending 20-year anniversary of Beatlemania in America;* LEFT COLUMN, BELOW *This Beatle interview album, THE BEATLES TALK DOWNUNDER (Raven Records, 1981), was issued two decades after the fact;* RIGHT COLUMN *The obscure THE BEATLES IN ITALY compilation LP (Parlophone Records), and THE ESSENTIAL BEATLES, a hard-to-come-by "greatest hits" package from Australia (Apple Records);* OPPOSITE PAGE *Same album, different cover:* TOP ROW, LEFT *THE HAMBURG TAPES VOLUME 2 (Breakaway Records, date unknown) and* (SECOND ROW, LEFT) *LIVE AT THE STAR CLUB (Bellaphone Records, 1977); two incarnations of the Beatles/Tony Sheridan tapes include* (TOP ROW, CENTRE) *THE BEATLES FEATURING TONY SHERIDAN (Pickwick Records, 1962) and* (SECOND ROW, CENTRE) *VERY TOGETHER, Canada (Polydor Records, 1969). This latter jacket is significant in its symbolic depiction of Paul McCartney's alleged demise. Issued during the "Paul is Dead" fervour of 1969, the startling image of one of the four lights of the Beatles prematurely snuffed out was just too much for some record retailers who refused to carry the otherwise tame album;* TOP ROW, RIGHT *The original Beatles' YESTERDAY AND TODAY and its controversial first incarnation* (SECOND ROW, RIGHT) *known popularly as "THE BUTCHER COVER" (both Capitol Records, 1966);* THIRD ROW, LEFT *MEET THE BEATLES, Capitol's premiere Beatle LP in America (1964) and* (BOTTOM ROW, LEFT) *the equivalent release in Canada;* THIRD ROW, RIGHT *MAGICAL MYSTERY TOUR, Germany (Apple Records, 1967) and its American counterpart below (1967).*

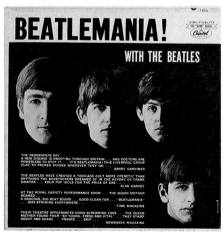

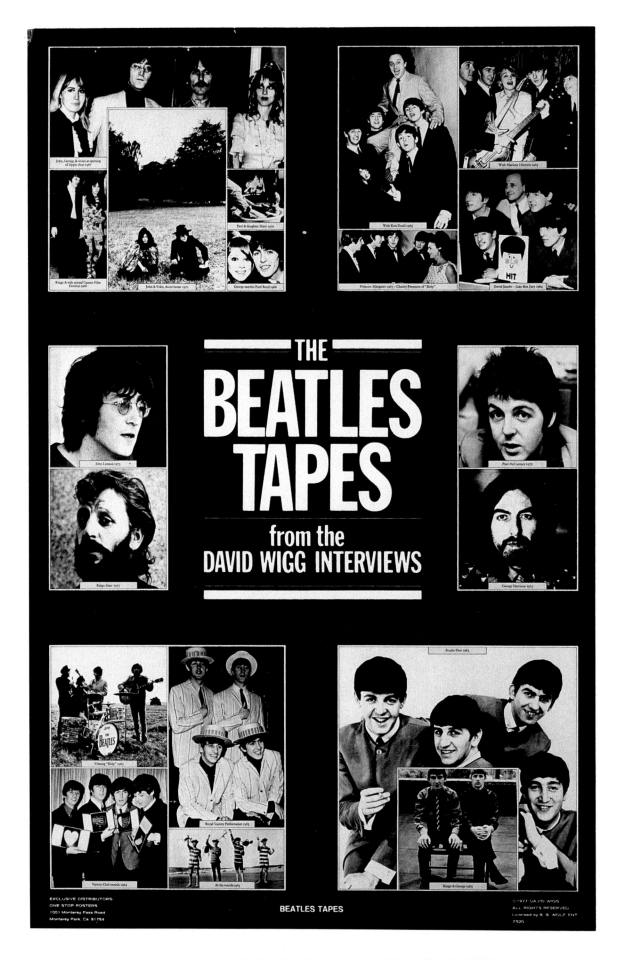

*An in-store poster hawking* THE BEATLES TAPES *(Polydor Records, 1976).*

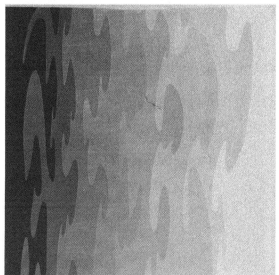

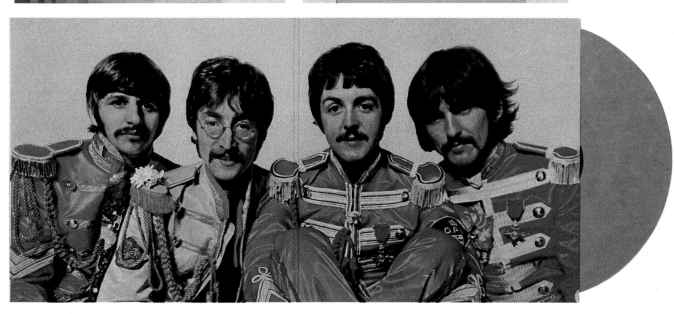

*The original SGT. PEPPER stem to stern:* **TOP ROW** *The back cover, and the fabled front cover;*
**SECOND ROW** *The record sleeve designed by the Dutch artists known collectively as The Fool, and the
psychedelic cut-out insert by project director Peter Blake;* **BOTTOM** *The flashy inside gatefold portrait
of the popular "act we've known for all these years" (Capitol Records, 1967).*

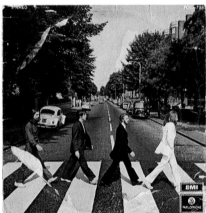

**TOP ROW** *An extremely rare British copy of the "WHITE ALBUM" with the records inserted from the top rather than the sides as was the norm (Apple Records, 1968);* **SECOND ROW** *Three of the Beatles' final original releases:* ABBEY ROAD *(Parlophone Records, 1969); the first real group compilation of any merit known both as the* BEATLES AGAIN *and* HEY JUDE *(Apple Records, 1970), and the Beatles Fan Club only release* THE BEATLES CHRISTMAS ALBUM *(Apple Records, 1970).*

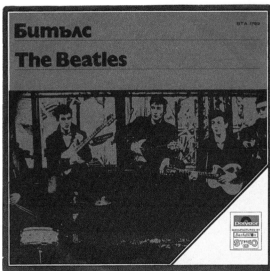

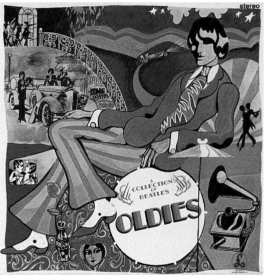

*Beatle-related releases from around the globe:* TOP *The Japanese* RARITIES *(Odeon Records, date unknown);* SECOND ROW THE BEATLES *hailing from Bulgaria (Polydor Records, date unknown); A* COLLECTION OF BEATLES OLDIES *(Parlophone Records, 1966);* BOTTOM ROW TWIST AND SHOUT *from Canada (Capitol Records, 1964), and back to Germany where it all began with* LIVE AT THE STAR CLUB *(Lingasong Records, 1977).*

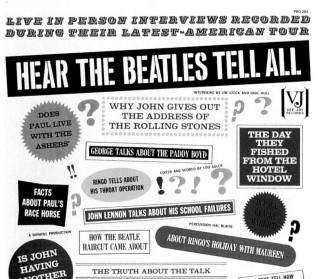

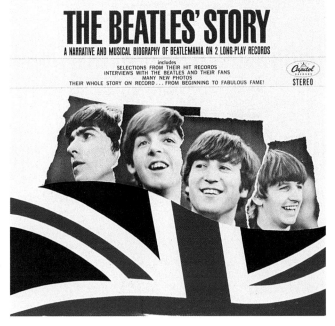

*It wasn't only the Beatles' music that captivated a generation, but what they had to say. Four examples of so-called "Beatle speak" LPs:* **TOP ROW** HEAR THE BEATLES TELL ALL *(Vee Jay Records, date unknown);* THE MCCARTNEY INTERVIEW *(Columbia Records, 1980);* **BOTTOM ROW** *British journalist David Wigg's insightful* THE BEATLES TAPES *(Polydor Records, 1976) and finally* THE BEATLES' STORY *issued originally during the height of Beatlemania (Capitol Records, 1964).*

TOP ROW *Original newspaper ad promoting the double album* THE BEATLES;
SECOND ROW *A pristine page of label graphics for the Beatles'* LOVE SONGS *compilation.*

**TOP ROW** *The Beatles'* 20 GREATEST HITS *alongside its classy inner sleeve (Capitol Records, 1982);* **SECOND ROW** *The inside gatefold to* RARITIES *(Capitol Records, 1980);* **BOTTOM ROW** *The Beatles'* ROCK AND ROLL MUSIC VOLUME I *next to the promotional radio station release of the same album (Capitol Records, 1976).*

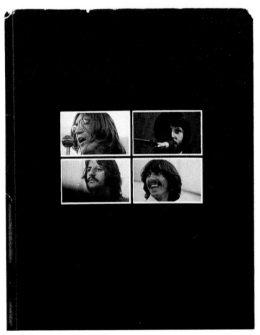

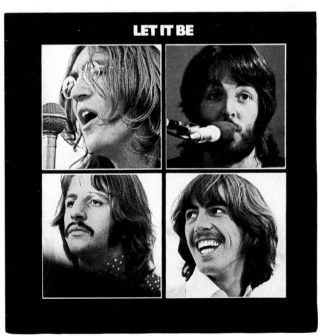

*The hard-to-find LET IT BE boxed set consisting of not only the record, but a stunning picture book of the historic recording sessions, photographed by American photographer Ethan Russell, with transcripts of dialogue from the film (Apple Records, 1970).*

**ABOVE** *Lennon winds down at the press party celebrating the release of* SGT. PEPPER, *1967;*
**BELOW** *George Harrison in the early seventies.*

ABOVE *Ringo showing off on the accordion at Apple's swank offices on Savile Row;*
BELOW *Whaling away on drums during Wings' first days together.*

**ABOVE** *Taping a 1964 British television show;* **OPPOSITE PAGE, ABOVE** *With temporary Ringo replacement drummer Jimmy Nicol in 1964;* **OPPOSITE PAGE, BELOW** *Sgt. Pepper's Lonely Hearts Club Band onstage at Brian Epstein's Saville Theatre on Shaftesbury Avenue, London, during filming for a promotional short for the tune "Hello Goodbye." Note Ringo's ridiculous miniature drum kit.*

OPPOSITE PAGE, ABOVE *The psychedelic Beatles pose together, early in their Apple days;* OPPOSITE PAGE, BELOW *Posing in the park, 1966;* BELOW *In profile, 1967;* BACKGROUND *The quiescent Liverpool skyline where the Beatles' magnificent music was born.*

# 2

# SHIRLEY'S WILD ACCORDION

## SOLO LPS

**T**oo many people lost touch with the Beatles following the last garish blast of Beatlemania in the late sixties and therefore missed much of the amazing post-Beatles potpourri of sights and sounds. As John Lennon once told me: "The Beatles were only a prelude to the music we are making now as individuals. It was an invaluable education certainly. But school's out now and it's time to get out there and make it on our own. The only thing left is to move forward. That's the only real challenge for us now, the only future we have any right to expect. We make the music we want, without having to look over our shoulders all the time."

Like all serious artists, the Beatles cherished their creative freedom and when the curtain finally fell on the group they were each determined to successfully go it alone. This was something their millions of fans often found very difficult either to accept or embrace. Even after John Lennon's sad passing in 1980, Ringo complained that he was *still* getting badgered by people wondering when the Beatles would play together again. "When there's only

**OPPOSITE PAGE** *"Watching Rainbows, A Fine Natural Imbalance." Serigraph by the author, 1978.*

one of us left, I'm sure they'll still be asking."
Beatle dreams, it seems, die hard.

In contemplating the extraordinary solo careers of John Lennon, Paul McCartney, George Harrison and Ringo Starr one is struck by the quantity, range and variety of the music each artist made while a member of the Beatles and after the group disbanded in 1970. From John and Yoko's late-sixties' *Two Virgins* to George's Indian-influenced *Wonderwall*, McCartney's little-known instrumental remake of the eccentric *Ram* (released under the peculiar pseudonym of Percy "Thrills" Thrillington), and Ringo's quirky, country-inspired *Beaucoups of Blues*, all of the Fabs vigorously exercised their musical independence by steadfastly writing and recording to suit their tastes. Important, too, was the desire to package their records in their own style, rather than that of some Establishment, money-mad record company.

Years later, John remembered the original concept behind the controversial nude cover for *Two Virgins* (1968): "We were both a bit embarrassed when we peeled off for the picture. So I took it myself with a delayed action shutter. That was to prove we were not a couple of demented freaks, we were not deformed in anyway and our minds were healthy. If we can make people accept these things without offence, without sniggering, then we shall be achieving our purpose . . . . If people can't face up to the fact of other people being naked or smoking pot, or whatever they want to do, then we're never going to get anywhere."

Other solo albums, too, bore the distinctive mark of their creators. Lennon's *Mind Games* and *Walls and Bridges* both showcased his original artwork while Paul designed the covers of *Wild Life* and *Ram*. Never far behind, Ringo illustrated a scene from his early days with an impressive photo montage for the sleeve of his schmaltzy *Sentimental Journey* and George took a shot at recording his impressions of Apple's energetic press office with a painting he did for the experimental album *Electronic Sound*.

With other projects the Beatles often conceived the idea for the sleeve, then left it to the record company's art department to actualize the finished illustration. Paul recalls his original concept behind the cover of his award-winning *Band on the Run*. "We were just laying in bed one night, thinking what shall we use for the album cover? Why not a group of people caught in a spot light as if they're trying to escape from jail? First, we thought we would use actors, and then we figured no, that's not really going to mean much. Let's try and get different people who are personalities themselves from various walks of life. [American film actor] James Coburn is in there and so is John Conteh, a boxer from Liverpool – a few different people [including British talk-show host Michael Parkinson], just for a lark."

Linda McCartney, who married Paul in March 1969, has often been involved in producing photography for her husband's work, contributing covers for the albums *McCartney* and *McCartney II*, as well as *Ram*, *Red Rose Speedway*, *Tug of War*, and *Pipes of Peace*, among others. John and Yoko also shot a cover or two. Yoko, for instance, took the now famous Polaroid photo of John which adorns his masterwork *Imagine*, while Lennon snapped Ono for the cover of her avant-garde double album *Fly*.

Sometimes it wasn't just a visual idea that took centre stage on the boys' solo album jackets, but a "philosophical" one. Take the

*A vintage graphic for the album* Wings at the Speed of Sound.

case of George Harrison's *Living in the Material World*. Here the spiritual Beatle boldly proclaimed his newly focused love of the great blue god Krishna by including a full-colour painting of his heart's desire on the enclosed lyric sheet. In 1971, during the height of Lennon and McCartney's famous feud, Paul, too, made a telling visual comment on his album *Ram* by including a tiny photo of one real live beetle literally caught in the act of screwing another.

All things considered, the solo LPs of the former Fabs display a remarkable degree of versatility and originality, sometimes rivalling even the group's collective works for their musical intensity and sheer creative brilliance. Certainly compositions like John's "Imagine," McCartney's "Mull of Kintyre" and Harrison's "What is Life" will remain standards in the tradition of such Beatles classics as "Yesterday" and "All You Need is Love." While perhaps not as well remembered, the graphic statements made by the four will likewise survive, mirrored in the near constant reissues released in various forms regularly around the world.

*A beautifully designed 3-D in-store stand-up for Wings' eclectic swan song* BACK TO THE EGG.

*A rare promotional mobile for George Harrison's* THIRTY THREE & ⅓.

**ABOVE** *A promotional poster for Wings' "Junior's Farm" single (Apple Records);*
**BELOW** *Wings official 1979 Christmas card. Note Denny Laine (second from left) wishing*
*everyone a merry Christmas by slyly slipping fans the finger.*

**TOP TO BOTTOM** *The inside gatefolds for George Harrison's* LIVING IN THE MATERIAL WORLD
*(Apple Records, 1973);* DARK HORSE *(Apple Records, 1974); and finally,*
THIRTY THREE & 1/3 *(Dark Horse Records, 1976).*

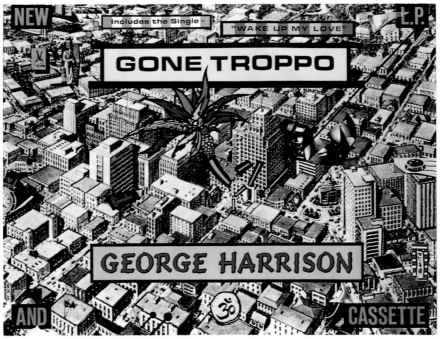

ABOVE LEFT *Harrison high on* CLOUD NINE *in this 1988 graphic;* ABOVE RIGHT GONE TROPPO'S *North America promo poster signed by designer "Legs" Larry Smith;* BELOW *Artist Larry Smith's limited-edition promotional poster for George's 1982 critical and commercial flop* GONE TROPPO.

ABOVE *Wings all gussied up to promote their "Goodnight Tonight" single (Parlophone Records, 1979);* BELOW *The entire McCartney/Wings catalogue to 1978 as seen in this promotional piece for* WINGS GREATEST.

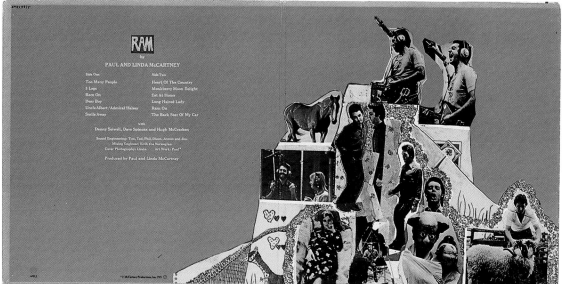

*The inside gatefold graphic for three of McCartney's finest solo efforts;* **TOP TO BOTTOM** MCCARTNEY
*(Apple Records, 1970);* RAM *(Apple Records, 1971);* RED ROSE SPEEDWAY *(Apple Records, 1973).*

*The inside covers of Paul McCartney's most popular works:* **TOP TO BOTTOM** VENUS AND MARS
*(Capitol Records, 1975); the triple album* WINGS OVER AMERICA *(Capitol Records, 1976);*
MCCARTNEY II *(Columbia Records, 1980).*

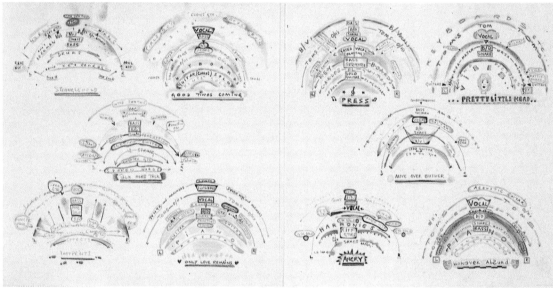

*More McCartney inside album covers for:* **TOP TO BOTTOM** CONCERTS FOR THE PEOPLE OF
KAMPUCHEA (Atlantic Records, 1981); PRESS TO PLAY (Capitol Records, 1986); GIVE MY
REGARDS TO BROADSTREET (Columbia Records, 1984).

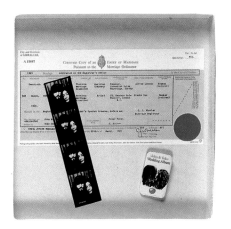

*John and Yoko's eccentric WEDDING ALBUM (Apple Records, 1969). Although the graphics and design were spectacular, the record itself was significantly less appealing, showcasing the couple's unique vocal talents by calling each other's names back and forth over the entire first side of the LP.*

*A striking advertisement for John and Yoko's MILK AND HONEY released following the former Beatle's tragic assassination (Polygram Records, 1984).*

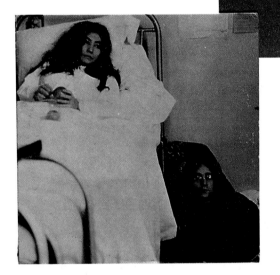

**TOP ROW** *The front and back covers to John and Yoko's controversial* UNFINISHED MUSIC NO. 1:
TWO VIRGINS *(Apple Records, 1968);* **CENTRE** *The album's "plain brown wrapper" in-store cover;*
**BOTTOM ROW** *The front and back covers to their uninspired* UNFINISHED MUSIC NO.2:
LIFE WITH THE LIONS *(Zapple Records, 1968).*

ABOVE *The moody free poster included inside George Harrison's majestic triple album boxed set*
ALL THINGS MUST PASS; **BELOW** *The clever front covers to* JOHN LENNON PLASTIC ONO BAND
*(Apple Records, 1970) and* YOKO ONO PLASTIC ONO BAND *(Apple Records, 1968).*

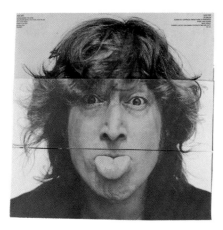

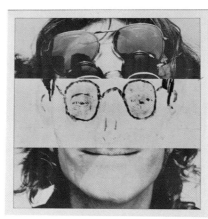

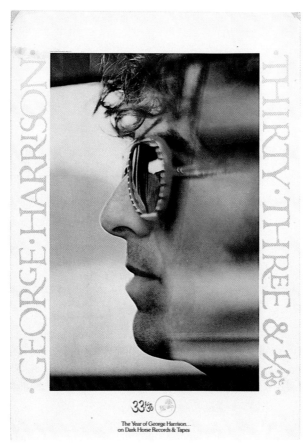

TOP ROWS *The amusing back cover and inserts from Lennon's* WALLS AND BRIDGES
*(Apple Records, 1974);* BELOW *A tasteful ad for George Harrison's* THIRTY THREE & ⅓.

*The extravagant press kit for McCartney's* PRESS TO PLAY.

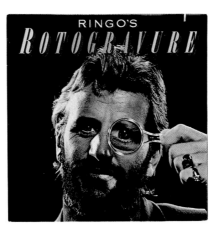

*Ringo Starr's solo albums:* **TOP ROW** GOODNIGHT VIENNA *(Apple Records, 1974);*
RINGO'S ROTOGRAVURE *(Atlantic Records, 1976);* RINGO THE 4TH *(Atlantic Records, 1977);*
**SECOND ROW** BAD BOY *(Portrait Records, 1978); the last Apple LP ever,* BLAST FROM YOUR PAST
*(1975);* RINGO *(Apple Records, 1973);* **BOTTOM ROW** STOP AND SMELL THE ROSES *(Boardwalk
Records, 1981);* BEAUCOUPS OF BLUES *(Apple Records, 1970); and the difficult-to-find Canadian
release* OLD WAVE *(RCA Records, 1983).*

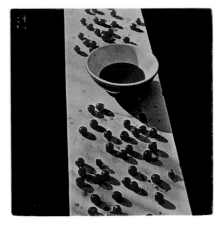

*The cream of Paul McCartney's solo work:* **TOP ROW** M<small>C</small>C<small>ARTNEY</small> (*Apple Records, 1970*);
R<small>AM</small> (*Apple Records, 1971*); W<small>ILD</small> L<small>IFE</small> (*Apple Records, 1971*); **SECOND ROW** R<small>ED</small> R<small>OSE</small> S<small>PEEDWAY</small>
(*Apple Records, 1973*); B<small>AND</small> <small>ON THE</small> R<small>UN</small> (*Columbia Records, 1973*); V<small>ENUS AND</small> M<small>ARS</small> (*Capitol
Records, 1975*); **BOTTOM ROW** W<small>INGS AT THE</small> S<small>PEED OF</small> S<small>OUND</small> (*Capitol Records, 1976*);
W<small>INGS</small> O<small>VER</small> A<small>MERICA</small> (*Capitol Records, 1976*); L<small>ONDON</small> T<small>OWN</small> (*Capitol Records, 1978*).

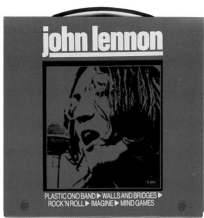

*Two John Lennon boxed sets issued after the composer's death. The specially manufactured boxes are pictured on the top row (CENTRE AND RIGHT). The blue carrying case is made of plastic and was issued only in Greece, the silver box in Great Britain. The albums shown are: TOP LEFT IMAGINE (Apple Records, 1971) autographed by Lennon's half sister, Julia Baird; SECOND ROW MIND GAMES (Apple Records, 1973); LIVE PEACE IN TORONTO (Apple Records, 1969); WALLS AND BRIDGES (Apple Records, 1974); BOTTOM ROW SOMETIME IN NEW YORK CITY (Apple Records, 1972); ROCK AND ROLL (Apple Records, 1975), and SHAVED FISH (Apple Records, 1975).*

SOLO LPS

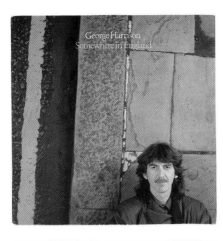  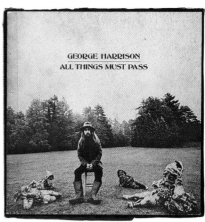

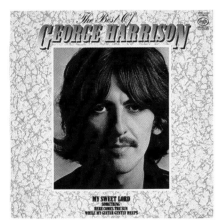  

*Same record, different jacket:* **TOP ROW, LEFT** *Somewhere in England* (Dark Horse Records, 1981) *and* (**SECOND ROW, LEFT**) *its original unreleased cover (1980);* **TOP ROW, CENTRE** *Dark Horse* *(Apple Records, 1974) and* (**SECOND ROW, CENTRE**) *a 1974 re-release from England's Music for Pleasure Limited;* **TOP ROW, RIGHT** *All Things Must Pass* (Apple Records, 1970) *and* (**SECOND ROW, RIGHT**) *the same album as issued in Japan (Toshiba EMI, 1970);* **BOTTOM ROW, LEFT TO RIGHT** *The Best of George Harrison, a re-release also from Music for Pleasure, the American issue (Capitol Records, 1976) and the original English version (Capitol Records, 1976).*

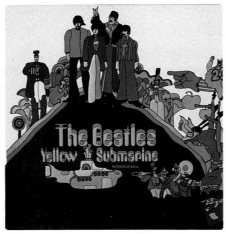

Beatle-related soundtrack albums: **TOP** *The expanded inside gatefold for Rapple Records'* SON OF DRACULA *starring Harry Nilsson and Ringo Starr (1974);* **SECOND ROW** LIVE AND LET DIE *title track by Paul McCartney and Wings (United Artists Records, 1973); The Beatles'* YELLOW SUBMARINE *(Apple Records, 1969);* THE MAGIC CHRISTIAN *starring Peter Sellers and Ringo Starr, with music by Paul McCartney and the Apple band Badfinger (Apple Records, 1970);* **BOTTOM ROW** WATER, *a Handmade Film with a live musical sequence featuring George Harrison and Ringo Starr (Decca Records, 1985);* OH! CALCUTTA! *with a small vignette written by John Lennon (Aidart, 1969);* **OPPOSITE PAGE, TOP LEFT** *A Canadian point of purchase placard for* MILK AND HONEY; **TOP RIGHT** *A rare promotional poster for the album* GEORGE HARRISON; **BELOW** *Uncut record labels from Wings'* SPEED OF SOUND, *George's* ALL THINGS MUST PASS *and Wings'* LONDON TOWN.

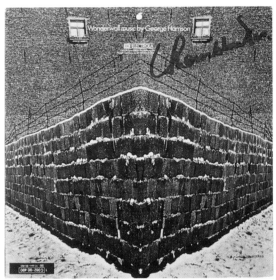

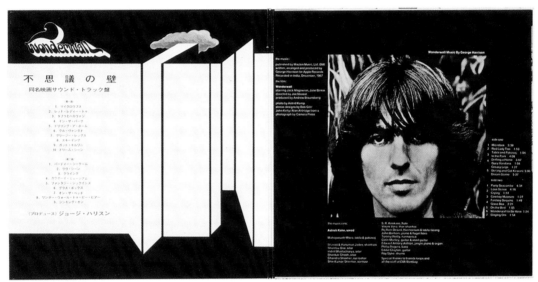

TOP ROW *George Harrison's solo* WONDERWALL *(Apple Records, 1968) and its graphically innovative back jacket autographed by Harrison's sometime sitar instructor, Shambu Das;* SECOND ROW *The inside gatefold of the deluxe Japanese edition of* WONDERWALL *(Apple Records, 1968);* BOTTOM ROW *Harrison's* ELECTRONIC SOUND, *both the front and back covers are from original acrylic paintings done by George (*LEFT *Italy, Zapple Records, 1972;* RIGHT *Zapple Records, 1969).*

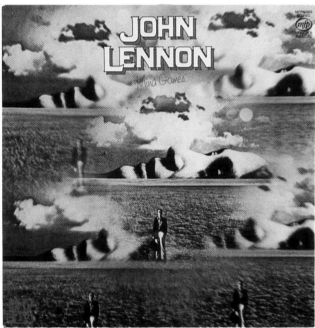

**TOP RIGHT AND LEFT COLUMN** *The Plastic Ono Band's* LIVE PEACE IN TORONTO *as nature intended it, with the original free 13-month calendar insert included in the album's first issue. What happened, you might ask, if you only owned an old eight-track player back then? You simply filled out the postcard included in your* LIVE PEACE *eight-track cartridge and, within a few fast weeks Apple would deliver a calendar to your door (Apple Records, 1969);* **BOTTOM LEFT** *One of the very few occasions where a record company actually improved on the artist's original cover concept:* MIND GAMES *(Music for Pleasure Records, 1973).*

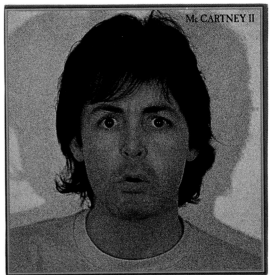

**TOP ROW** *Beatle George takes a walk along the back covers of his* GEORGE HARRISON *(Dark Horse Records, 1979) and* SOMEWHERE IN ENGLAND *LPs (Dark Horse Records, 1981);* **SECOND ROW** *Paul McCartney albums:* BACK TO THE EGG *with Wings (Capitol Records, 1979);* MCCARTNEY II *(Columbia Records, 1980) and* **(BOTTOM)** TUG OF WAR *(Columbia Records, 1982).*

**ABOVE** *The inside open gatefolds to John and Yoko's* SOMETIME IN NEW YORK CITY
*(Apple Records, 1972) and* **(BELOW)** MILK AND HONEY *(Polygram Records, 1984).*

*The Lennons selling peace in Canada, 1969.*

 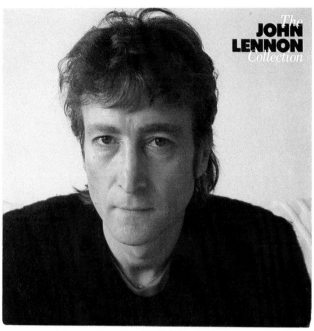

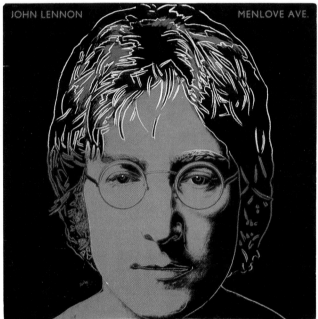 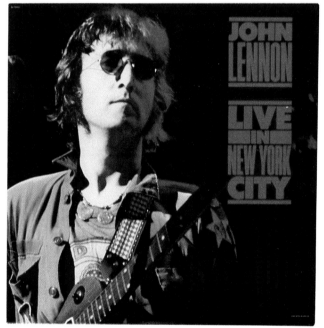

*Lennon's last four albums:* **TOP ROW** *MILK AND HONEY (Polygram Records, 1984);*
*THE JOHN LENNON COLLECTION (Geffen Records, 1980);* **BOTTOM ROW** *MENLOVE AVENUE*
*(Capitol Records, 1986) and LIVE IN NEW YORK CITY (Capitol Records, 1986).*

*The ins and outs of George Harrison's* EXTRA TEXTURE: **TOP ROW** *The entertaining album's imitation orange plastic-look front and back cover;* **BOTTOM ROW** *The cheeky cardboard record holder and the back cover showing a smiling George out on the road in 1974 (Apple Records, 1975).*

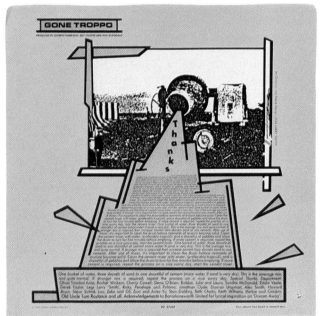

*The ins and outs of* GONE TROPPO: **TOP ROW** *The wildly eccentric front and back cover;*
**BOTTOM ROW** *The informative liner bag front cover explaining the recipe for mixing cement,*
*and the illustrated lyric sheet on the bag's opposite side (Dark Horse Records, 1982).*

*Beatle-related charity albums:* **ABOVE** No One's Gonna Change Our World, *perhaps the first all-star ecology album featuring an unreleased version of the Beatles' "Across the Universe" (Starline Records, 1970);* **BELOW** Greenpeace *(A&M Records, 1985) Compiled to aid the controversial environmental watchdog group, the LP contains a remixed and edited version of George Harrison's "Save the World," originally included on his* Somewhere in England *(Dark Horse Records, 1981).*

THRILLINGTON, *an orchestrated cover of Paul McCartney's* RAM *masterminded by the former Beatle under the pseudonym Percy Thrillington (Capitol Records, 1977).*

OPPOSITE PAGE *Paul McCartney is an extremely proficient musician, having mastered several instruments including bass, guitar, clarinet, trumpet and, as witnessed here, drums;* ABOVE *The Beatles during the heady heights of Beatlemania.*

LEFT *Relaxing on the lawn of their rented Bel Air mansion during a well-deserved respite from the rigours of touring, September 18, 1965;* BELOW *On the banks of the River Thames in London, 1969;* BACKGROUND *Lennon's alternate boyhood home, his mother Julia's house on Blomfield Road in the Liverpool suburb of Springwood. As a boy, Paul McCartney also spent time here, jamming with his boyhood musical partner.*

# 3

# INDIAN ROPE TRICK

## BOOTLEGS

ootleg recordings, whether by the
Beatles or anyone else, present an
important dilemma to the serious
collector of this obscure, histori-
cally significant music. Ripping off
any artist by issuing recordings
never intended for release represents, at best,
a rather significant offence against good man-
ners and, at worst, a legally and ethically crimi-
nal act.

For the sincere Beatle aficionado, however,
almost every alternate take, studio blunder,
unfinished demo, live appearance or last-
minute rehearsal is considered sacred and
must be scrupulously tracked down and preserved with single-minded devotion.

If, as one suspects, the great work of the
Beatles secures a position in history along with
the esteemed classical composers of the past,
surely it behoves those closest to the actual
sequence of events to help chronicle every
last undone tune or wayward note left dan-
gling by the indiscriminate hand of time. That
the creators are shortchanged of royalties and
mechanical rights is simply an unfortunate
and unavoidable consequence of being too

**OPPOSITE PAGE** *This bootleg of the Beatles' 1968 "White Album"
(the Black Album) even duplicated the poster/lyric sheet insert.*

shortsighted to realize the true value of even their less polished material.

Far worse than any money-grubbing record company or unreasonably perfectionist musicians, however, are the naughty sound pirates themselves. Motivated not by any genuine philanthropic concern for the preservation of rare, unfinished works of art, they do what they do purely and simply for money. Lots of money. These days, the gross take on a popular illicit recording can easily net manufacturers well in excess of $200,000 to $300,000.

The very first bootleg this author ever saw was in a Tampa, Florida, head shop in 1970 and sold for a mere $6. Devoid of any appreciable album-cover graphics, this alternate compilation of already reasonably well-known material delivered pretty much what the photocopied sleeve promised: studio quality outtakes by the Beatles, recorded in London.

Today, however, matters aren't quite so straightforward. One favourite trick of the bootleggers is to put out an album, then later re-issue exactly the same material in a different jacket with a deceptive new title. By the time word gets around, literally tens of thousands of the bogus boots have already been sold. Other, even sleazier types have been known to actually fake outtakes by erasing the vocal track on a regular release, adding a little extraneous background "studio noise," then claiming the finished product is a rare backing demo to one of the Fabs' famous tunes. Price-wise, too, modern day bootlegs are often excessive, with some poorly recorded, shoddily packaged double LPs selling at various conventions and swap meets for up to $150.

To be fair, however, there is another, more positive side to the thorny question of these "unofficial" releases. At their best, bootlegs offer collectors an opportunity to hear their favourite musicians perform in a whole new way. Free of the sometimes creatively restrictive constraints of so-called "serious" recording, artists often enjoy using the studio to experiment with new sounds, jam with friends or simply rehearse previously unreleased tunes. Finding their way onto record, this type

of off-the-cuff material can make for very exciting listening.

The single biggest trove of officially unreleased Beatles outtakes remains the 90-plus hours of largely unused soundtrack recordings from the 1969 film documentary *Let It Be.* Beginning January 2, the Beatles laid down more the 100 tunes on a gruelling 28-day schedule, conducted both at Twickenham Film Studios and the Beatles' own facility in Apple's cavernous basement on Savile Row. The group recorded a wide variety of songs, including reworked versions of classics such as "Love Me Do," "I'm So Tired," "Kansas City," the Everly Brothers' "Bye Bye Love," "Norwegian Wood," and "House of the Rising Sun," as well as such highly unlikely "secondary" material as "The Hare Krishna Mantra," "Michael Row the Boat Ashore," "You Are My Sunshine," and the sneaky theme from the film *The Third Man.* Interestingly, the four also taped several songs that later turned up on various solo projects including Lennon's biting "Gimme Some Truth," McCartney's "Teddy Boy" and Harrison's "All Things Must Pass."

These musical "work-outs," recorded when the band was at its freest and creatively most unencumbered ("What difference did it make what we did?" said Lennon later. "The group was already half dead by then anyway...") have served as the basis for more than 75 Beatle bootlegs. That's considerable mileage from music considered by the group to be, in Lennon's words, "throwaway" material.

Perhaps the most significant advance in recent years has been the introduction of bootleg compact discs into what is now a fiercely competitive market. When, for instance, George Harrison and Bob Dylan went onstage at Los Angeles' Palomino Club to join longtime friend Jesse Ed Davis on a couple of tunes, a pricey ($40 per disc) surreptitiously recorded CD entitled *The Silver Wilburys* began to turn up in record stores across North America within two weeks of the gig. "It makes you afraid to ever touch your bloody guitar again," a distraught

Harrison later commented. Other bogus CDs have also turned up from both Ringo and Paul's recent solo tours of the States.

Today's bootlegs are also of value for their interesting graphics. Free of any critical or copyright constraints, these hit-and-run operations are often managed by fanatical fans who go out of their way to include suitably rare images on their illicit products.

Material by the late John Lennon is perhaps the most consistently bootlegged, complete with professionally designed sleeves, beautiful, full-colour photos and even original drawings by the bespectacled Beatle. The next Beatle in order of bootleg popularity seems to be George, whose underground admirers have issued several of his more tuneful live record-ings, as well as many of the mystically inclined musician's multitude of unreleased demos. Strangely, bootlegs by the high-profile McCartney seem to run a distant third with the pirates, a popularity contest the money-conscious Paul is more than happy to lose.

Like it or not, bootlegs are an age-old rock 'n' roll tradition unlikely to fade away. For all their good and evil, one thing is certain: each time a major music figure takes the stage these days, you can be sure someone is hunched over a tiny, sophisticated recorder salting away all the good vibrations for future use. A bane for artists and record companies, bootlegs will continue to grow in stature and importance as long as people insist upon putting a price tag on music.

*Although the music inside the two-record BLACK ALBUM (EVA Records, date unknown)*
*is totally different, the album cover art is the reverse mirror image of the original.*

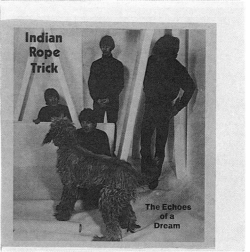

*Early Beatle bootlegs. With their utilitarian approach to design and generally poor sound quality, these vintage recordings harken back to a less sophisticated time when you could enjoy the so-called "extra, unreleased" work of your favourite artist for a mere five or ten bucks. Sold almost exclusively through head shops, this is where it all began:* TOP ROW 20 x 4 *(Ruthless Rhymes Records, 1971);* INDIAN ROPE TRICK *(Fan Records, date unknown);* SECOND ROW BYE BYE BYE SUPER TRACKS 1 *(Contra Band Records, 1970), the first illicit recording ever owned by the author;* BOTTOM ROW BEATLES *(Contra Band Records, date unknown) and* FROM US TO YOU, A PARLOPHONE REHEARSAL SESSION *(producer unknown, 1975).*

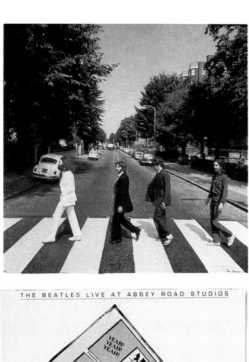

*ABBEY ROAD outtake albums:* **TOP ROW** *RETURN TO ABBEY ROAD (no information available), an exact replica of the original except that the Fab Four seem to be walking in the opposite direction; NO. 3 ABBEY ROAD (no information available), including a rare McCartney/Donovan duet recorded in the late sixties;* **SECOND ROW** *THE BEATLES LIVE AT ABBEY ROAD (no information available), created when a particularly inventive fan snuck a tiny plastic tape recorder into a special open house at the famous studios in 1983 and taped portions of the master recordings that were played; Two LET IT BE period bootlegs, IN A PLAY ANYWAY (Circuit Records, date unknown) and* **(BOTTOM ROW, LEFT)** *SWEET APPLE TRAX (Newsound Records, 1975);* **BOTTOM ROW, RIGHT** *THE REAL CASE HAS JUST BEGUN (Core Records, 1986).*

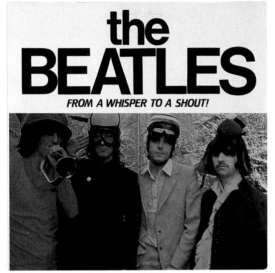

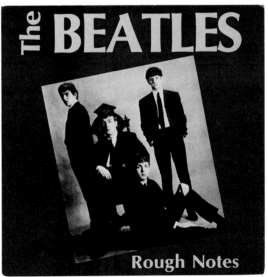

*Beatle bootlegs issued almost ten years after the boys went their separate ways:* **TOP ROW** BROADCASTS
*(Circuit Records, 1980);* FOUR SIDES, *a lively two-record set (EVA Records, date unknown);* **SECOND
ROW** FROM A WHISPER TO A SHOUT! *(no information available);* GREAT TO HAVE YOU WITH US
*(Jet Records, date unknown);* **BOTTOM ROW** SILVER LINING *(Midwest Records, 1979), and*
ROUGH NOTES *(no information available).*

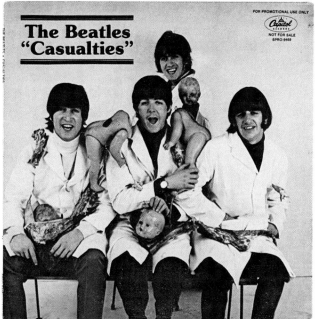

*Several years back it was rumoured that Capitol Records intended to release a compilation of alternate mixes, takes and other assorted recorded rarities. They never did, but the ever-obliging bootleggers were ready to take up the slack, as with these three gems:* **TOP** COLLECTOR'S ITEMS *(no information available);* **BOTTOM ROW** NOT GUILTY *(EHMV Records, 1985), and* CASUALTIES *(no information available).*

*Twenty years of Beatle bootlegs:* **TOP ROW** *The bizarre cover for the almost legitimately released 1969 Beatle single "What' a Shame Mary Jane had a Pain at the Party" (no information available); a collection of high-quality studio outtakes of "Strawberry Fields Forever" by the Cadillac of bootleggers, NEMS Records;* **BOTTOM ROW** LIVE AT THE HOLLYWOOD BOWL *(Pod Records, date unknown) with a porcine Paul depicted as the pig-headed culprit who broke up the Beatles;* NOT FOR SALE *(no information available), another NEMS package featuring previously unreleased numbers such as "Leave my Kitten Alone," "Shout" and "How Do You Do It."*

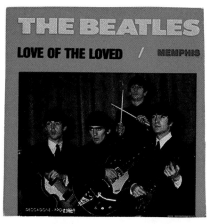
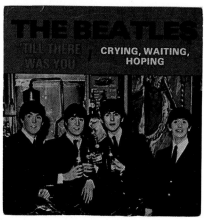

*They may look like the real thing but they're not: 45 picture covers for yet another incarnation of the endlessly bootlegged 1962 Decca audition tapes. Here the naughty record pirates have tried to make their product look similar to the official Beatle Capitol releases issued throughout the sixties.*

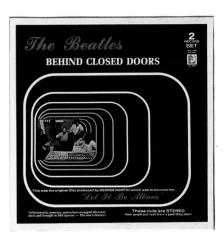

TOP ROW *These 1980s releases fall somewhere between bootlegs and legitimate releases;* THE BEATLES AND THE ROLLING STONES *(Joker Records, 1973), heart-stopping live performances by the two legendary bands;* THE BRITISH ARE COMING *(Silhouette Records, 1982), a novel 3-D Beatles album complete with freaky blue-and-red plastic viewing specs;* BEHIND CLOSED DOORS *(Moonchild Records, date unknown), the Beatles oft-pirated 1969 Twickenham Studios* GET BACK *sessions trotted out yet again, this time as a deceptively legitimate-looking record;* SECOND ROW *Three pirated live Beatle performances:* FIVE NIGHTS IN A JUDO ARENA *(De Weintraub Records, date unknown), perhaps the first full-colour bootleg ever;* LIVE FROM THE SAM HOUSTON COLOSSEUM *(Audifon Records, 1973), a similar offering; and finally* VANCOUVER 1964 *(Ruthless Rhymes Records, 1971);*
BOTTOM ROW *Back covers of second row albums.*

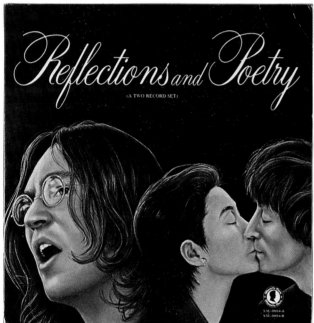

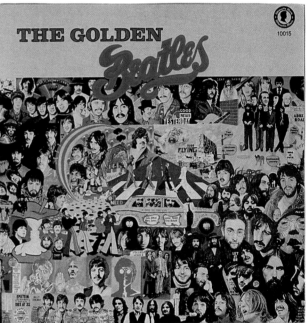

**ABOVE** LIVE RECORDINGS (*Wizardo Records, date unknown*), *a mid-seventies rehash of Lennon's fabled live Madison Square Garden concert;* **BELOW** *While it's unfair to actually call these interesting Silhouette Records releases true bootlegs, they do tend to straddle the line by including recordings to which the rights are somewhat vague. Rumour has it the Lennon-based* REFLECTIONS AND POETRY *(1984) was the subject of a legal action between the small Brooklyn based label and notorious litigator Yoko Ono; and* THE GOLDEN BEATLES *(1985).*

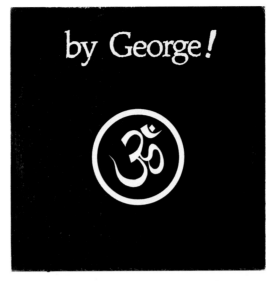

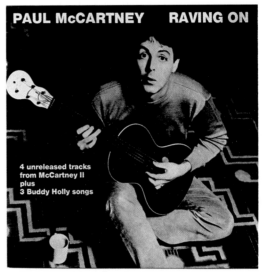

*Solo Beatle bootlegs:* **TOP ROW** *Illicit compilations of the music of George Harrison:* ONOTHIMAGEN *(Loka Records, 1987), a well-designed, musically interesting two-record set;* BY GEORGE! *(Handmade Records, date unknown) and finally* **(SECOND ROW, LEFT)** UNDERSIDE *(Underside Records, 1979);* **SECOND ROW, RIGHT** RAVING ON *(Sandwich Records, 1985), an uneven collection of several Wings-era McCartney outtakes;* **BOTTOM ROW** PAUL MCCARTNEY IN SCOTLAND *(Wizardo Records, 1975), an unauthorized recording from the Beatle's initial 1973 Wings European tour; and* SUITABLE FOR FRAMING *(no information available).*

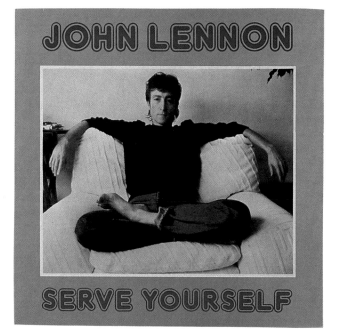

**TOP ROW** THE ROCK AND ROLL CIRCUS *(Barking Moose Records, date unknown), featuring a rousing rendition of "Yer Blues" from the unaired 1969 live performance by Eric Clapton, Keith Richards, Jimi Hendrix' drummer Mitch Mitchell and John;* JOHN LENNON TELECASTS *(no information available), a collection of Lennon's various television performances;* **BOTTOM ROW** SERVE YOURSELF *(Love & Peace Records, 1984), John's unreleased, ingenious, off-the-cuff answer to Bob Dylan's overtly religious "Gotta Serve Somebody" (from Dylan's 1979 release* SLOW TRAIN COMING*);* JE SUIS LE PLUS MIEUX, *a 15-minute studio outtake of Lennon rehearsing "I'm the Greatest", a song which eventually surfaced as a Ringo Starr tune on the popular* RINGO *album.*

*John Lennon bootlegs:* **ABOVE** YIN YANG *(Bag Records, date unknown);*
**BELOW** TEDDY BOY *(Midwest Records, 1979).*

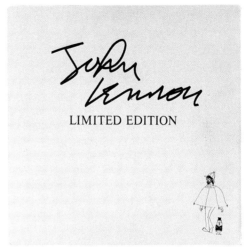

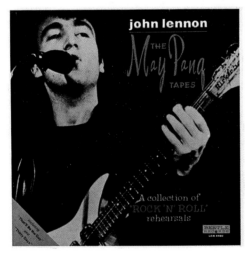

TOP ROW *A HARD ROAD* (Moriphon Records, date unknown), some final musical memories from the great maestro; *LIMITED EDITION* (Bag Records, date unknown), an interesting assortment of Lennon oddities from the last two decades of his turbulent, eventful life; SECOND ROW *THE WILLOWBROOK REHEARSALS* (Blackbird Records, 1986), a pricey two-record bootleg of the Beatle's musical meanderings with Apple's Elephant's Memory band during an off-the-cuff series of rehearsals in 1972; *YOU SHOULD 'A BEEN THERE* (no information available), a collection of high quality outtakes from the Phil Spector-produced *ROCK AND ROLL SESSIONS*; BOTTOM ROW The tongue-in-cheek title of this popular eighties bootleg is *THE MAY PANG TAPES* (Beetle Records, date unknown) named for John's other Oriental girlfriend during his infamous 18-month estrangement from Yoko; in *GOODNIGHT VIENNA* (Dakota Records, 1985) Lennon croons an early version of a tune composed for his old pal Ringo.

**TOP ROW** *Something Precious & Rare (Blackbird Records, 1986), a late-eighties bootleg featuring original artwork by John Lennon; Off the Walls (no information available), John's original demos for his 1974 Walls And Bridges LP;* **BOTTOM ROW** *Snap Shots (Gnat Records, 1984), a mediocre assortment of unreleased Lennon material from his final years; Before Play (Gnat Records, 1984).*

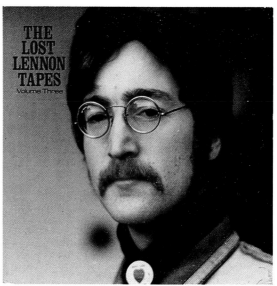
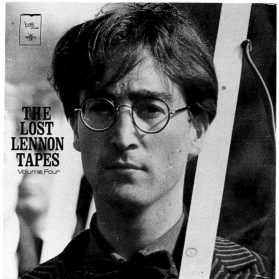

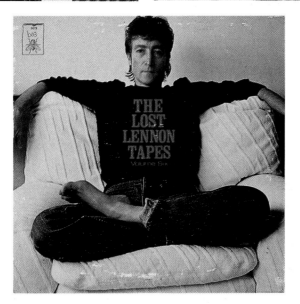

*Part of the extended series of pirated recordings from the Westwood One Radio series*
*THE LOST LENNON TAPES (Bag Records, 1988), produced eight years after John's death.*

TOP *"Beatle Peace," a fanciful collage by the author (1989);* BOTTOM *A mid-eighties Lennon bootleg,* Winston O'Boogie, *trading on the late Beatle's self-ascribed pseudonym, Dr Winston O'Boogie.*

**TOP ROW** *You know you've really made it when you merit your very own bootleg. The UFO Records release* JULIAN LENNON, *front and back (date unknown);* **BOTTOM ROW** THIS IS NOT HERE, *front and back, Yoko Ono's only bootleg to date (Bag Records, date unknown).*

**ABOVE** *At the celebrated "Bed-in for Peace" in Amsterdam, March 25, 1969;*
**BELOW** *Hard at work together at Abbey Road, 1969.*

*Flying high in a rare onstage performance, February 9, 1974.*

STRAWBERRY
FIELD

COPY of an ENTRY of BIRTH
PERSUANT to the BIRTHS & DEATHS ACT

Registration District Liverpool in the County of Lancashire

TOP LEFT *John and Julian at Heathrow Airport in London, prior to boarding a plane for a holiday in Greece, July 22, 1967;* BOTTOM LEFT *John holds up a facsimile copy of his birth certificate at Apple, 1969;* BOTTOM RIGHT *Lennon as a cheeky washroom attendant in the 1967 British television special* NOT ONLY BUT ALSO; BACKGROUND *Strawberry Fields, the single most sacred spot to Beatle fans around the world.*

# 4

# THINKING OF LINKING

## SINGLES, EPS AND PICTURE COVERS

Twenty-five years ago, the release of a new Beatles single was a treat for fans everywhere. Today most people prefer the superior sound quality and relative ease of playback offered by compact discs and cassettes. This isn't to say that singles no longer have a place in today's world of superlative audio technology. Indeed, for the serious aficionado their appeal remains strong, both for the honest way they convey the energetic essence of rock 'n' roll and for their classic sleeve designs. The 45 rpm picture cover remains one of the most important pieces in the cultural legacy left by the group. Even a casual examination of these striking graphics allows one to trace the Beatles' colourful creative evolution and to gain a sense of the wide spectrum of music they produced.

Another prominent collectible to Beatle people is the controversial seven-inch extended play recording popularly known as the EP. For the uninitiated, an EP is like an ordinary single except that it is usually played at 33⅓ rpm and contains up to three cuts per side as opposed to the single's meagre one. To this day, many American record company

*An original oil painting of James Paul McCartney by noted artist Frank Poole.*

bigwigs have generally resisted its production in the United States, favouring instead long-playing albums and 12-inch maxi-singles. The precise reason why is anyone's guess, but one supposes it must have something to do with the fact that giving the consumer an extra two or three tunes on what is basically a single tends to cut down sales of both the conventional LP and the two-song 45.

While *Magical Mystery Tour*, the soundtrack to the Beatles' 1967 television special, was issued as a two-EP set in Great Britain and other parts of the world, it was unceremoniously relegated to one side of a standard album in the United States and Canada. The other side was filled out with the Fabs' single releases from the past year including "Strawberry Fields Forever" and "Hello, Goodbye." This gave the Americans a full-fledged new Beatle LP to flog, a much preferable and more profitable commodity than the EP. Today, as fate would have it, the original British two-record package and booklet have become highly collectible, as have many other mid-sixties EPs issued by the band.

For potential collectors, singles and EPs offer a good place to start to build one's personal Beatles library. Still reasonably inexpensive enough to be within range of most fans, a whole treasure trove of rare pressings remain available to the keen Beatle consumer at rummage sales, church bazaars and used record stores (not to speak of Mom and Pop's attic). The trick is to know what you are looking for. Rare pieces like Apple's *Walls Ice Cream* EP (valued today at upwards of $300), the sought-after Hamburg-era Beatle 45 "My Bonnie" ($700 or more for a mint copy) or the obscure and valuable Wings' single "Walking in the Park with Eloise" (actually an instrumental written by Paul's father Jim, and released under the pseudonym of the Country Hams) can still be found mixed in with other less exciting finds.

Now that we've firmly and forever entered the high-tech age of supersound reproduction via both compact and laser discs, the future of the seven-inch single seems admittedly dim.

Though realistically we can't really hope for too many more new releases, it is encouraging for both Beatles fans and collectors that existing singles are increasing in both value and prestige.

"Personally, I always liked Beatle music best on 45s," George Harrison confided to this author during a late 1983 interview at his home in Henley, Oxfordshire. "It's really a pity they seem to be on the way out. Sometimes I think we just bang along too fast for our own good, leaving behind some of the best and simplest things as we go."

Even more than the singles and EPs themselves, it is their unique sleeves which tend to attract enthusiasts. Unlike the Beatles' LPs, which were generally similar in design from country to country, the seven-inch covers varied widely with a whole series of wild, imaginative graphics produced to help market both the group's collective and solo work. Often big-name artists and photographers like Alan Aldridge, Roy Kohara, "Legs" Larry Smith, Ethan Russell, Richard Avedon, Robert Freeman, John Kosh, Aubrey Powell, Dezo Hoffmann and even the Beatles themselves would contribute their talents to the various designs, assuring a whirling panorama of colourful images to please even the most particular hardcore fans. "We always spent a hell of a lot of time overseeing our single sleeves," John Lennon told me during a meeting with the former Beatle in Syracuse, New York. "Paul and I especially. That's not to say we always had the cooperation of the record companies. There were lots of rows over the photos we wanted and shit like that. But that's an old story. It's always a fight to try and do something good. Paul, especially, was great at getting what he wanted. I'd either just lose interest or charge right in, thereby pissing everyone off."

In today's big business world of rock 'n' roll collectibles, the now all-but-commercially dead seven-inch single is still big news to memorabilia buffs. It's strange to think that something that originally sold for pennies now brings the kind of serious money it does. I

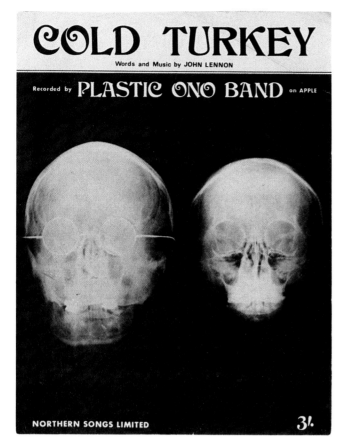

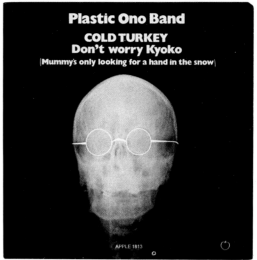

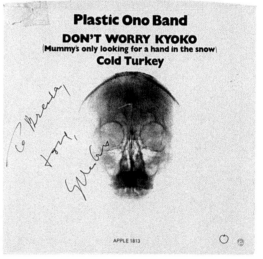

remember one well-known, big-league Beatle dealer from Ohio, Scott Rubin, saying that if he could somehow travel back in time all he would want to do was visit a typical, small-town Woolworths, circa 1964. "Think of all the great Beatle stuff they'd have, man," he chuckled, playfully smacking himself on the forehead at the thought.

For the committed collector, it seems the prospect of scoring a pristine condition "Ticket To Ride" picture sleeve or an original set of four Beatles bubble bath figures is tantamount to winning the New York lottery. And according to what I've seen over the years, probably much more of a long shot.

*Leave it to John and Yoko to come up with something as deeply original as having their own skulls x-rayed and then slapping them on a record:* **TOP LEFT** *The highly collectible sheet music for "Cold Turkey";* **RIGHT, TOP TO BOTTOM** *The hard-to-find single and a graphically reversed bootleg picture cover, autographed by Yoko Ono, for "Cold Turkey's" warbly B side "Don't Worry, Kyoko, Mummy's Only Looking for a Hand in the Snow." And finally, two heads are better than one on this obscure Japanese pressing.*

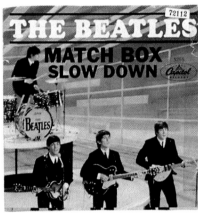

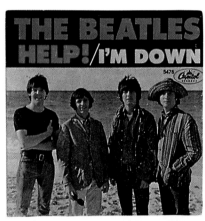

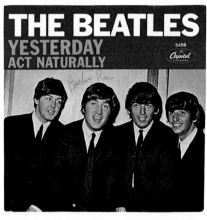

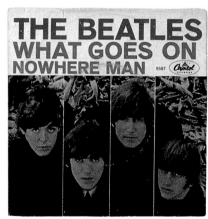

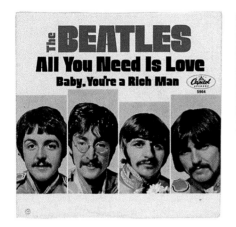

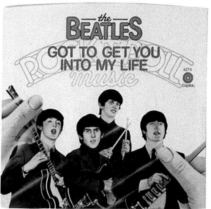

*Beatle picture covers from the United States. With the exception of (OPPOSITE PAGE, TOP LEFT)
"Love Me Do," which was a Tollie Records release, the remainder of these tasty collectibles were all
issued by Capitol Records.*

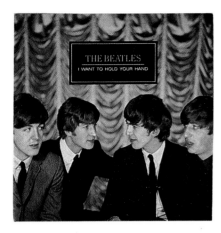

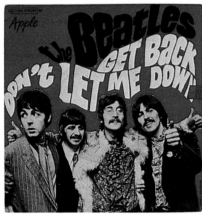

*Beatle picture covers:* **TOP ROW** *"I Want to Hold Your Hand" (Parlophone Records,
date unknown); "Ain't She Sweet" (Polydor Records, date unknown); "Lady Madonna"
(EMI Records, date unknown);* **SECOND ROW** *"Get Back" (Apple Records, 1969); "All You Need is
Love" (Apple Records, date unknown); "Sgt. Pepper's Lonely Hearts Club Band" (EMI Records, date
unknown);* **BOTTOM ROW** *"Ain't Nothin' Shakin' Like the Leaves on a Tree" (Collectables Records,
date unknown); "All You Need is Love" (Parlophone Records, 1967)*

*Beatle picture covers;* **TOP ROW** *"Back in the USSR" (Odeon Records, 1968); "Ob-La-Di, Ob-La-Da" (Apple Records, date unknown); "Get Back" (Apple Records, 1969);* **SECOND ROW** *"Hey Jude" (Odeon Records, date unknown); "Red Sails in the Sunset" (Collectables Records, date unknown).*

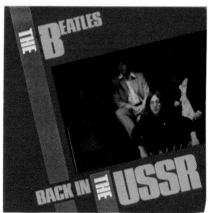
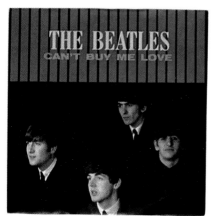

**OPPOSITE AND ABOVE** *A few years back, in an effort to reverse what was judged to be a slump in sales of the Beatles' formerly lucrative singles catalogue, marketing experts reasoned that if they repackaged the old tunes with an updated look, the cash registers might once again begin to clatter away (Parlophone).*

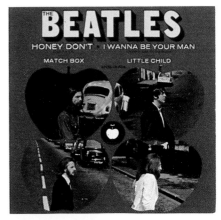

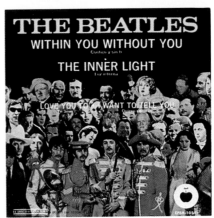

*Beatle EPs from around the world:* **TOP ROW** *"Misery" (Odeon, 1964); "Please Please Me" (Odeon, 1964); "Long Tall Sally"*
*(Parlophone, 1964);* **SECOND ROW** *"Yesterday" (Parlophone, 1965); "Help" (Parlophone, 1965); "Strawberry Fields Forever" (Odeon,*
*date unknown);* **THIRD ROW** *"Michelle" (Odeon, 1966); "Magical Mystery Tour" (Parlophone, 1967); "Honey Don't" (Apple, 1971);*
**BOTTOM ROW** *"Yellow Submarine" from Mexico (Apple Records, 1969); "Within You Without You" (Apple Records, 1971).*

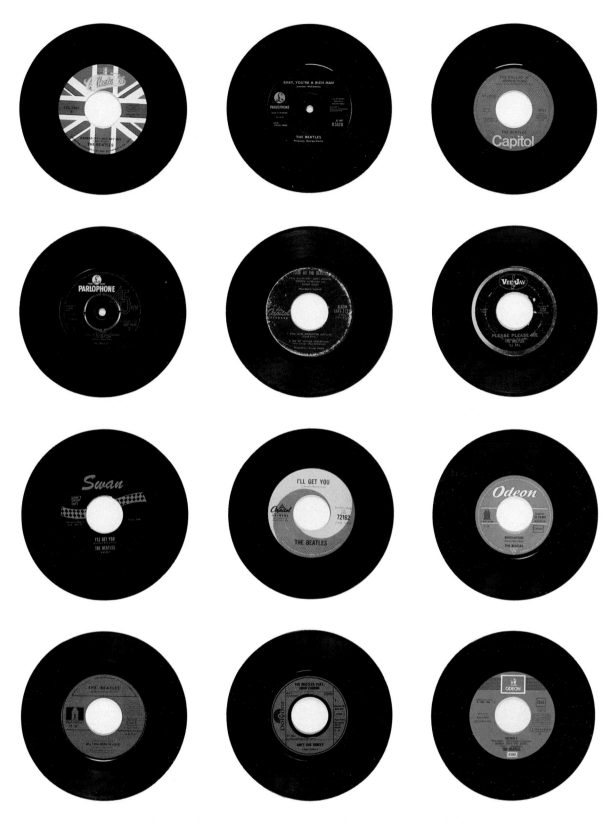

*Ever since the ground-breaking group first reached the zenith of the music business, over a dozen different labels have carried the prestigious imprint of the Beatles' name. A few prime examples:* **TOP ROW** *"Kansas City/Hey Hey Hey" (Collectables Records, date unknown); "Baby You're a Rich Man" (Parlophone Records, 1967); "The Ballad of John & Yoko" (Capitol Records, date unknown);* **SECOND ROW** *"Yesterday" (Parlophone Records, 1965); "Roll Over Beethoven" (Capitol Records, date unknown); "Please Please Me" (Vee Jay Records, date unknown);* **THIRD ROW** *"I'll Get You" (Swan Records, date unknown); "I'll Get You" (Capitol Records, 1964); "Revolution" (Odeon Records, date unknown);* **BOTTOM ROW** *"All You Need is Love" (Odeon Records, 1967); "Ain't She Sweet" (Polydor Records, 1961); "Misery" (Odeon Records, 1964).*

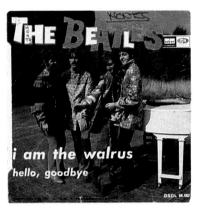
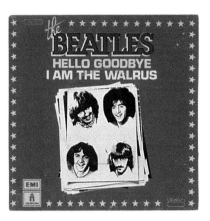

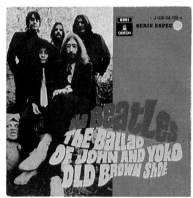

*Autour du monde avec les Beatles! Hard-to-find 45 picture covers from around the world:* **TOP ROW** *"All You Need is Love" (EMI Records, 1976); "I am the Walrus" (Odeon Records, 1967); "Hello Goodbye" (EMI Records, 1976)* **SECOND ROW** *"Back in the USSR" (EMI Records, 1968); "Ob-La-Di, Ob-La-Da" (EMI Records, 1976); "The Ballad of John and Yoko" (Odeon Records, 1969);* **THIRD ROW** *"The Ballad of John and Yoko" (EMI Records, 1976); "Beatles Forever," the generic all-purpose Canadian picture sleeve used to package several Beatle releases in the early seventies (Capitol Records); "Ballad of John and Yoko" (EMI Italy, 1976);* **BOTTOM ROW** *"Let it Be" (EMI Records, 1976); "Something" (Apple Records, 1969); and "Get Back" (EMI Records, 1976).*

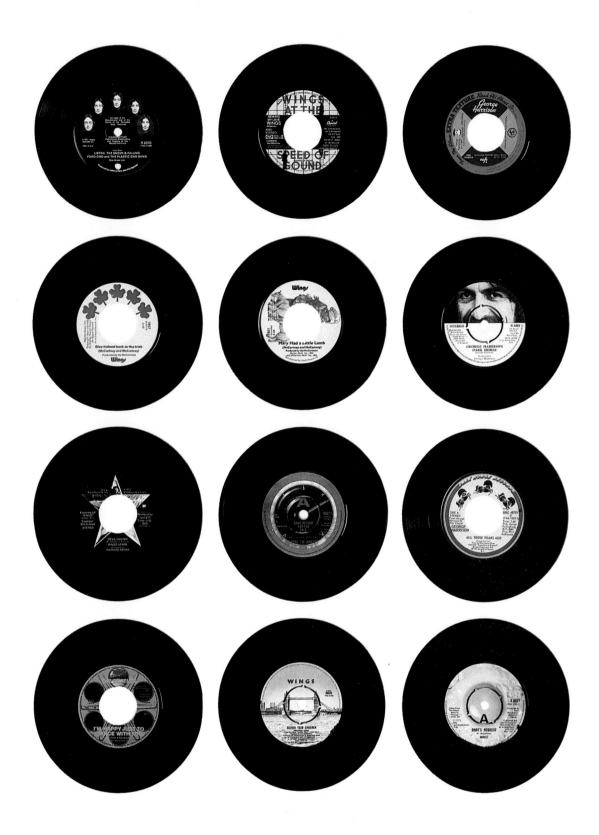

*The Beatles often rejected the standard, unimaginative record company label graphics in favour of a more personal, individualized look:* **TOP ROW** *John and Yoko's "Listen, the Snow is Falling" (Apple Records, 1971); Wings' "Beware My Love" (Capitol Records, 1976); Harrison's "You" (EMI Records, 1975);* **SECOND ROW** *Wings' "Give Ireland Back to the Irish" (Apple Records, 1972); McCartney's "Mary Had a Little Lamb" (Apple Records, 1972); Harrison's "Dark Horse" (EMI Records, 1974);* **THIRD ROW** *Ringo's "Devil Woman" (EMI Records, 1973); Wings' "Maybe I'm Amazed" (Capitol Records, 1976); Harrison's "All Those Years Ago" (Dark Horse Records, 1981);* **BOTTOM ROW** *The Beatles' "I'm Happy Just to Dance with You" (Capitol Records, 1982); Wings' "Deliver Your Children" (Capital Records, 1978); Wings' "Baby's Request" (Capital Records, 1969).*

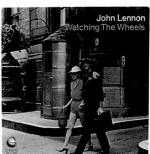

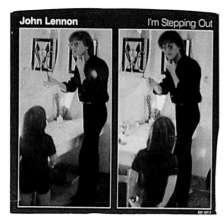  

*As graphically varied as they are musically absorbing, the global single releases of John Lennon have taken a well-deserved place in the forefront of popular music:* **OPPOSITE PAGE, TOP ROW** *"Give Peace a Chance" (Apple Records, 1969); "Mother" (Apple Records, 1970); "Instant Karma!" (Apple Records, 1970); "Instant Karma!" (Apple Records, 1970);* **OPPOSITE PAGE, SECOND ROW** *"Power to the People" (Apple Records, 1971); "Power to the People" (Apple Records, 1971); "Imagine" (Apple Records, 1971); "Imagine" (Apple Records, 1971);* **OPPOSITE PAGE, THIRD ROW** *"Woman is the Nigger of the World" (Apple Records, 1972); "Happy Xmas (War is Over)" (Apple Records, 1971); "Mind Games" (Apple Records, 1973); "Mind Games" (Apple Records, 1973);* **OPPOSITE PAGE, FOURTH ROW** *"I Saw Her Standing There" with Elton John and the Muscle Shoals Horns (DJM Records, 1975); "Stand By Me" (EMI Records, 1975); "#9 Dream" (EMI Records, 1974); "#9 Dream" (EMI Records, 1974);* **OPPOSITE PAGE, BOTTOM ROW** *"Beef Jerky" (EMI Records, 1974); "(Just Like) Starting Over" (Geffen Records, 1980); "Love" (Parlophone Records, 1970); "Watching the Wheels" (Geffen Records, 1981);* **ABOVE, TOP ROW** *"Instant Karma!" (Odeon Records, 1970); "Happy Xmas (War is Over)" (Odeon Records, date unknown); "Nobody Told Me" (Polygram Records, 1983);* **ABOVE, BOTTOM ROW** *"I'm Stepping Out" (Polygram Records, 1984); "Woman" (Geffen Records, 1981); "Two Minutes Silence," a wry conceptual bootleg (Antar Records, 1969)*

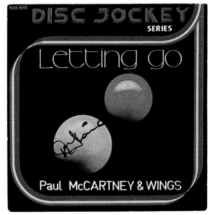

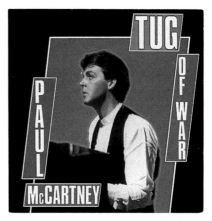

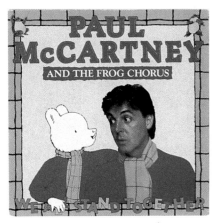

OPPOSITE PAGE *Of all the Beatles, Paul McCartney has showered the most attention on the packaging of his work. His innate design sensibility shows a love of rich illustration and tasteful presentation, as attested by this 20-year sample of 45 sleeves from around the globe:* TOP ROW *"Eat at Home" (Parlophone, date unknown); with Wings, "Live and Let Die" (Apple Records, 1973); "Letting Go" (Capitol Records, 1975);* SECOND ROW *"Jet" (Apple Records, 1973); "Letting Go" (EMI Records, 1975); released under the Wings pseudonym The Country Hams, "Walking in the Park with Eloise" (EMI Records, 1974);* THIRD ROW *Wings' "Maybe I'm Amazed" (Parlophone Records, 1977); "With a Little Luck" ( EMI records 1978); "I've Had Enough" (EMI Records, 1978);* BOTTOM ROW *"Stranglehold" (Capitol Records, 1986); the obviously unauthorized "Paul McCartney Talks About His Dear Friend John Lennon" (Fan Records, 1982);* ABOVE, TOP ROW *More Paul McCartney colourful 45s: "Getting Closer" (EMI Records, 1979); "Spin it On" (Columbia Records, 1979); McCartney solo work "Tug of War" (EMI Records, 1982);* ABOVE, BOTTOM ROW *"We All Stand Together" (Parlophone Records, 1984); "Spies Like Us" (Parlophone Records, 1985); "No More Lonely Nights" (Columbia Records, 1984).*

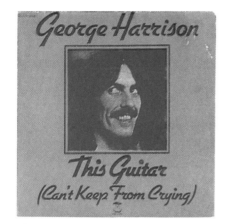

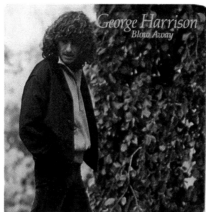

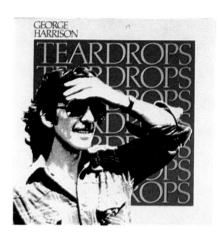

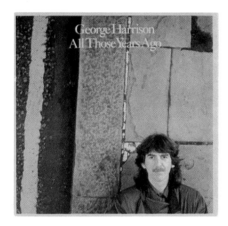

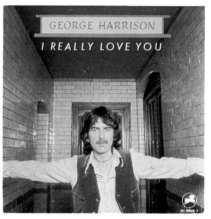

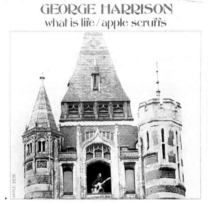

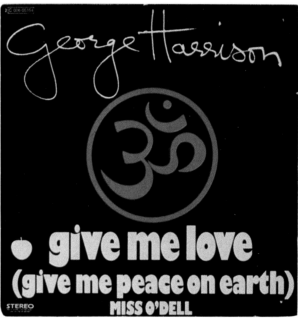

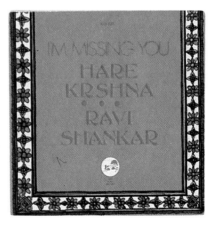

*The self-described dark horse of the group, the introspective George Harrison has enjoyed considerable success as a solo artist. A few of the musical mystic's international best:* **OPPOSITE PAGE, TOP ROW** *"This Guitar (Can't Keep From Crying)" (EMI Records, 1976); "Blow Away" (Dark Horse Records, 1979): "Teardrops" (Dark Horse Records, 1981);* **SECOND ROW** *"All Those Years Ago" (Dark Horse Records, 1981); "Wake Up My Love" (Dark Horse Records, 1982); "I Really Love You" (WEA Records, 1982);* **THIRD ROW** *"Dark Horse" (Apple Records, 1974); "What is Life" (Apple Records, 1970); "You" (Apple Records, 1975);* **BOTTOM ROW** *"Ding Dong; Ding Dong" (EMI Records, 1974); "Wake Up My Love" (Dark Horse Records, 1982); "My Sweet Lord" (Apple Records, 1970);* **ABOVE, TOP ROW** *Picture sleeves from around the world: "My Sweet Lord" (England, Apple Records, 1970); "My Sweet Lord" (Italy, Apple Records, 1970); "Bangla Desh" (place unknown, Apple Records, 1971);* **SECOND ROW** *"Bangla Desh" (USA, Apple Records, 1971); "Give Me Love (Give Me Peace On Earth)" (place unknown, Apple Records, 1973);* **BOTTOM ROW** *Three Krishna/Harrison-related singles: "Govinda" (Apple Records, 1970) by the Radha Krishna Temple; "Joi Bangla" (Apple Records, 1971) with sitarist Ravi Shankar and sarod virtuoso Ali Akbar Khan; "I'm Missing You" (Dark Horse Records, 1974).*

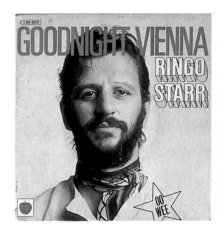

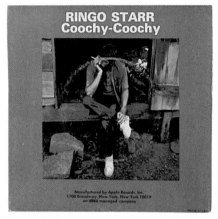

**OPPOSITE PAGE** *Though certainly not as prolific as his three super-talented cohorts, Ringo Starr also has had a few big hits in his time:* **TOP ROW** *"Goodnight Vienna" (EMI Records, 1975); "It Don't Come Easy" (Apple Records, 1971); "You're Sixteen" (EMI Records, 1973);* **SECOND ROW** *"Photograph" (Apple Records, 1973); "Snookeroo" (Apple Records, 1974); "Wrack My Brain" (Boardwalk Records, 1981);* **THIRD ROW** *"Only You" (Apple Records, 1974); "Coochy-Coochy" (Apple Records, 1970); "Oh My My" (EMI Records, 1973);* **BOTTOM ROW** *"Goodnight Vienna" (Apple Records, 1974), and "Back Off Boogaloo" (Apple Records, 1972);* **ABOVE** *George at the press launch for the Hare Krishna devotees' Radha Krishna Temple album released on Apple Records, 1970.*

**ABOVE** *The McCartneys chat with an old friend backstage after a 1976 Wings gig in Los Angeles;*
**BELOW** *Paul McCartney and Michael Jackson in the studio in the mid eighties.*

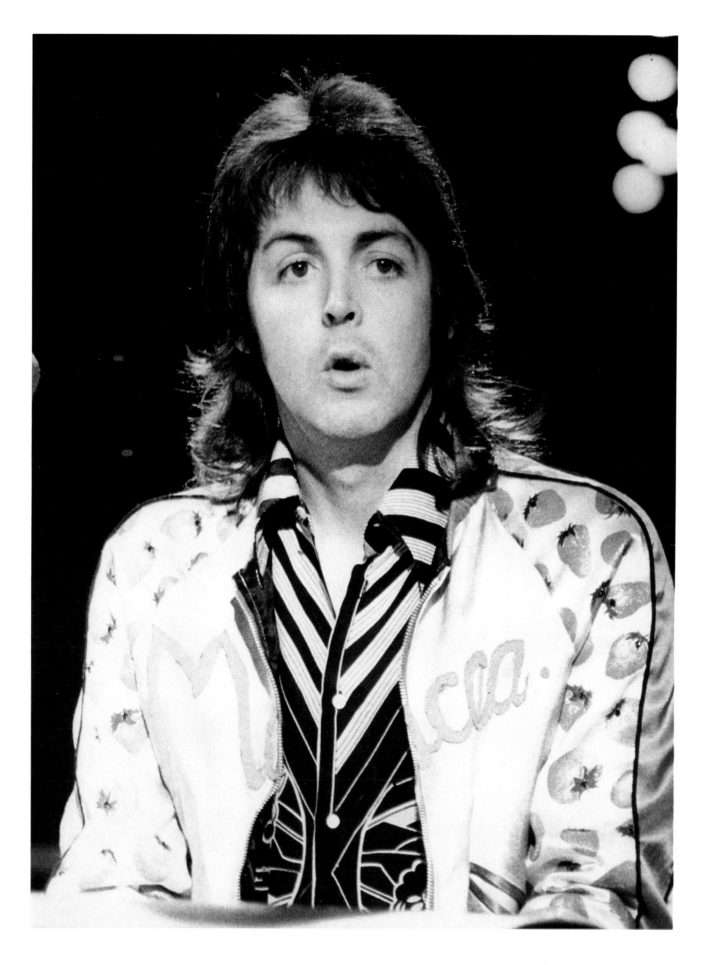

*Appearing on Britain's long-running TV staple "Top of the Pops" in the early seventies.*

**BELOW** *Beatle Paul and girlfriend, actress Jane Asher, at High Park Farm, McCartney's rural Scottish retreat near Campbeltown, Argyll, December 18, 1967;* **OPPOSITE PAGE** *Paul posing for photographers at his home, February 2, 1967;* **BACKGROUND** *Paul's one-time Liverpool home.*

# 5 FOUR NIGHTS IN MOSCOW

## ACETATES, FLEXI-DISCS, TAPES AND COMPACT DISCS

One of the most valuable of all Beatle-related collectibles is the rare and much sought-after acetate. Generally limited to a very exclusive run of just two or three copies, acetate discs hold a special appeal to collectors, since they were most often the personal property of the artists who recorded them. In addition, their plain unprinted labels often bore the handwriting of those same stars, thus offering great prestige to hardcore enthusiasts.

Acetates are cut in the mastering room of the studio as a courtesy to the artists, so they might have a chance to review their work outside the studio before recording is completed. Today, a quick cassette dub straight off the mixing board is generally the preferred method. Back when the Beatles were still rocking, however, these so-called demonstration discs were the industry standard. Because of their uniqueness, acetates are now impossibly chic among big-time collectors, with rare original Beatle compositions regularly fetching huge amounts at rock auctions on both sides of the Atlantic. Ironically, sometime Paul McCartney musical collaborator Elvis Costello owns a number of these desirable discs, as his

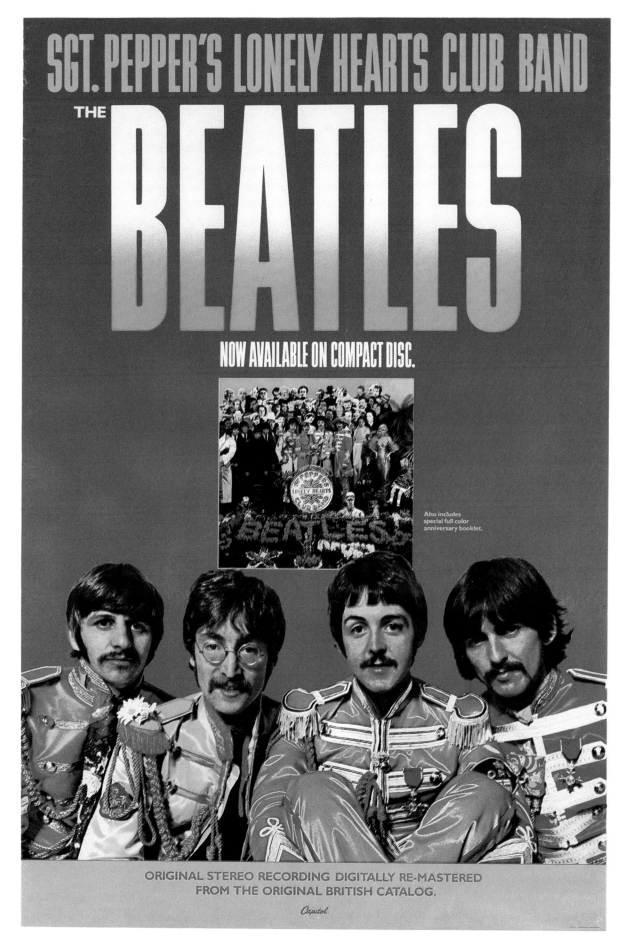

*The unflappable* SGT. PEPPER, *finally out on CD (Parlophone Records, 1987).*

father was associated with the Beatles' music publisher Dick James and had collected these demos in the course of his work.

Conversely, the humble flexi-disc (or soundsheet) may be easier to obtain, but still holds an undeniable attraction to fans for its sheer novelty and limited-edition status. Often distributed as special promotional items, these saucy seven-inch singles accommodated more off-the-wall, avant-garde type of material, as with the Beatles' yearly Fan Club Christmas records, today highly prized by Beatle buffs.

One flexi-disc worth special mention is the rare 1969 John and Yoko recording of their first miscarried child's heartbeat. It was included as part of a special subscription-only boxed set, produced in conjunction with the now-defunct *Avant Garde* magazine. More recently, in 1982, the Musicland record chain brought out a series of three red, white and blue promotional flexis marking Capitol Records' continuous attempts to keep the invaluable Beatle catalogue fresh in the minds of the record-buying public. These are also much sought after by collectors, priced upwards of $75 for the complete set.

Interestingly, all of these creatively diverse series of recordings were made by Eva-Tone Incorporated of Deerfield, Illinois. With the exception of another much smaller firm based in Britain, Eva-Tone was (and still is) the number one manufacturer of soundsheets in the world. By 1970, 100 million of these recordings had moved through Eva-Tone's presses, including several Beatle-related flexis never intended for public distribution, such as the group's 1968 message to Capitol Records' annual convention. Today the going price of that handout, if you're lucky enough even to find one, is a cool $3,000.

Another, somewhat more humble area of expertise for the sophisticated listener is the collecting of Beatle eight-track tapes, cassettes and compact discs. Over the years, a wide range of interesting and unusual tapes have been released by the group. These are collected today mainly for their unique packaging, rather than for the music.

A fairly recent newcomer to the already vast family of Beatle recordings is the high-tech compact disc, or CD. Commercially unavailable until February 1987, before that time only a very few of the increasingly popular releases ever found their way into the hands of fans, at least in America.

Now, of course, Beatle CDs are everywhere, but they are neither particularly interesting graphically nor collectible. That's not to say, however, that all compact discs are a dud as far as Beatle fans are concerned. Releases such as Paul McCartney's promotional "Birthday" single issued in 1990 and George Harrison's four-song CD included as part of his $500 book *Songs By George Harrison*, published by Britain's Genesis Publications, hold great promise as future collectibles. Other regular CD releases will probably never attain memorabilia status because they were issued in such great numbers so long after the fact. The music contained within, however, is masterfully wrought and impeccably presented.

While certainly not the solid mainstream collectibles that records and other memorabilia have become, flexis, tapes and CDs are still important to the "completist." If, over the next few years, sound technology continues to undergo rapid change, both CDs and cassettes may well go the way of eight-tracks, and be replaced by another as yet unimagined new method of reproduction. When and if these products are developed you can be sure fans everywhere will be hot on the trail of these chic "new" collectibles and paying good money for them.

 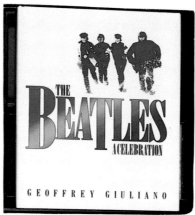 

  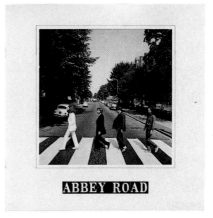

*With the advent of the technologically superior compact discs came a lot of interesting marketing and design opportunities. Packaged like miniature platinum records in their see-through plastic jewel cases, CDs provided a design field far different from the old-fashioned, oversized LPs or bulky eight-tracks.* **TOP ROW** *A rare numbered Japanese three-CD boxed set of* ABBEY ROAD, LET IT BE *and* MAGICAL MYSTERY TOUR, *complemented by a limited-edition enamel pin* **(TOP RIGHT)** *and* **(CENTRE)** *a built-in copy of this author's first book* THE BEATLES: A CELEBRATION; **SECOND ROW** *A special commemorative CD package of* ABBEY ROAD *complete with* **(RIGHT)** *an interesting, well-researched history of the work,* **(CENTRE)** *a specially manufactured pin and the classic album (EMI Records, 1987);* **BOTTOM ROW** *The incomparable* SGT. PEPPER'S LONELY HEARTS CLUB BAND *remixed, remastered and repackaged with a deluxe new lapel pin* **(CENTRE)**, *the original* SGT. PEPPER *cut-out insert* **(RIGHT)**, *a seven-page booklet (not shown), and a surprising alternate cover shot* **(LEFT)** *adorning this beautifully put together box (EMI Records, 1987).*

TOP LEFT *The deep blue ghost of George Harrison fades in and out of focus on this 1989 package of the composer's "greatest hits" (Dark Horse Records);* RIGHT COLUMN, TOP ROW *This posh, strictly limited-edition five-song CD – only 2500 copies were made – was included in the $500-plus book* SONGS BY GEORGE HARRISON, *issued by Britain's Genesis Publications;* RIGHT COLUMN, SECOND AND THIRD ROWS *Two rare compact discs: the well-designed CD single for the Traveling Wilburys' "Nobody's Child" (Wilbury/Warner, 1990) and a special promotional copy of Paul McCartney's live "Birthday" culled from his 1989–90 world tour (Capitol Records, 1990);* OPPOSITE PAGE *Some fine examples of the graphic pot-pourri available on Beatle-related CDs:* TOP ROW THE SILVER BEATLES, *a twangy collection of the ancient Decca audition tapes featuring ousted original drummer Pete Best (Overseas Records, 1982);* EVERY MAN HAS A WOMAN, *an assortment of songs composed by Yoko Ono and performed by such artists as Roberta Flack, Eddie Money and Elvis Costello (Polygram Records, 1984);* SECOND ROW *Linda McCartney's interesting still-life works well to cover the mishmash of mismatched melodies on Paul McCartney's forgettable* PIPES OF PEACE *(Columbia Records, 1983); John Lennon's memorable performance at a 1972 benefit in aid of mentally handicapped children, in league with the deeply together Elephant's Memory band (EMI Records, 1986);* BOTTOM ROW *A pirated bootleg copy of Paul McCartney's Soviet bloc rocker* BACK IN THE USSR *(Hocus Pocus Records, 1989); and finally, pop prophet Bob Dylan and former Fab George Harrison team up with greats Roy Orbison, Tom Petty and Electric Light Orchestra refugee Jeff Lynne on* THE TRAVELING WILBURYS VOLUME ONE, *a razor's edge assortment of torch ballads and searing melodies (Warner/Wilbury Records, 1988).*

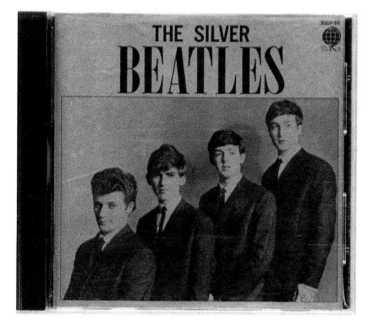

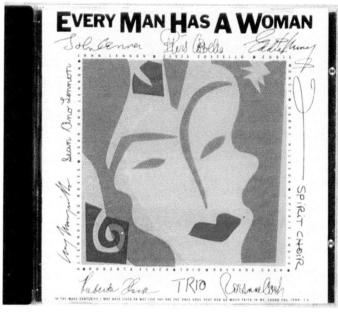

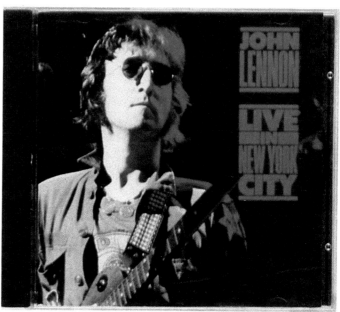

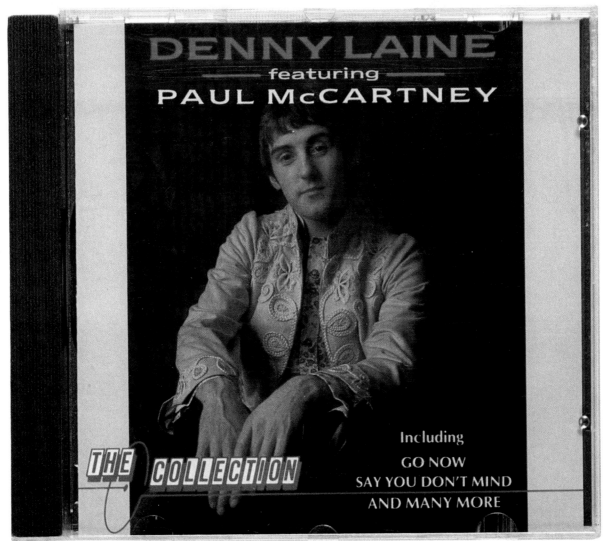

**ABOVE AND OPPOSITE PAGE, TOP** *A limited-edition CD record boxed set for McCartney's* FLOWERS IN
THE DIRT *(Parlophone Records, 1989) and the "free" mini CD included in the deluxe package;*
**OPPOSITE PAGE, BOTTOM** *A rare solo Denny Laine compact disc (Object Enterprizes, date unknown).*

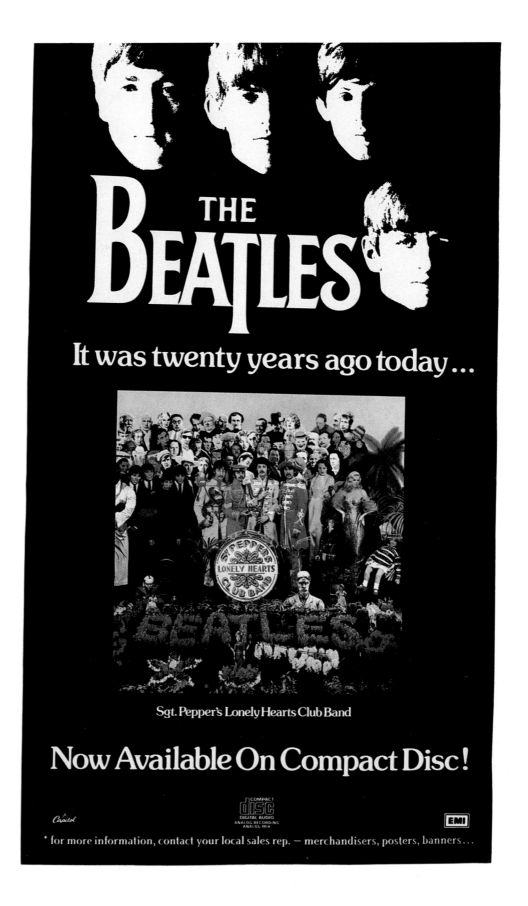

*Advertising the Beatles on CD.*

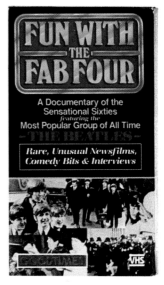

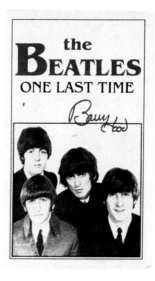

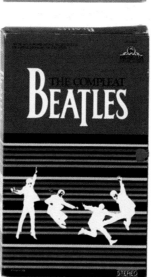
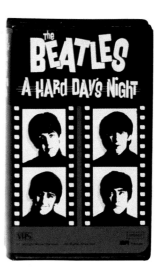

*And now the Beatles and friends on video in your own home – the best of what we've seen so far.*

*Four exceptional coloured flexi-discs given away as a special Capitol Records promotion by the American record store chain Musicland in 1982, now highly prized collectibles:* **TOP ROW** *GERMAN MEDLEY and 1962–1966;* **BOTTOM ROW** *ROCKY RACCOON and 1967–1970.*

*The fabled and valuable Christmas singles issued originally only to members of the Beatle Fan Club. These intriguing little records provide a private peek into the fascinating lives and times of Messrs. Lennon, McCartney, Harrison and Starr. For all their previous finely crafted, heartfelt music, here are the Beatles as pie-throwing, soft-shoe shuffling, British music hall comedians. As surreal as they are genuinely funny, the Christmas singles remain a significant key to unlocking the largely unexplored, Monty Pythonesque side of the Fab Four:* TOP ROW *"Another Beatles Christmas Record" (Parlophone Records, 1964); "The Beatles Third Christmas Record" (Parlophone Records, 1965);* SECOND ROW *"The Beatles 1968 Christmas Record" (Americom Corp., 1968); "Everywhere it's Christmas" (Parlophone Records, 1966);* BOTTOM ROW *"The Beatles Sixth Christmas Record" (Apple Records, 1968); "The Beatles Seventh Christmas Record" (Apple Records, 1969).*

ABOVE *A highly prized collection of Wings acetates from the vaults of Abbey Road Studios, cut by studio engineers at the end of a session for the artist. If these discs happen to contain any unreleased tracks or significantly altered versions of well-known tunes, they can be worth hundreds or potentially thousands of dollars to the collector;* CENTRE *A typical acetate or demostration disc mailing cover;* OPPOSITE PAGE *Beatle-related promotional singles:* TOP ROW *McCartney and Jackson's "Say Say Say" (Columbia Records, 1983); "Coming Up" (Columbia Records, 1980); "John Lennon on Ronnie Hawkins The Long Rap" (Cotillion Records, 1969);* SECOND ROW *"This Song" (Dark Horse Records, 1976); "It Happened" (Geffen Records, 1981); "All Those Years Ago" (Dark Horse Records, 1981). These "white label" promo discs were regularly sent out to both radio stations and reviewers in hopes of catching the attention of the ever fickle music media;* BOTTOM *The "Dark Horse" on stage during his ambitious 1974 North American tour.*

*Sometimes the packaging of a musical work becomes ultimately more important that the sounds contained within. An assortment of either extinct or obscure records and tapes:* **LEFT TO RIGHT, TOP ROW** *The handsomely designed box containing the cassette version of Harrison's majestic ALL THINGS MUST PASS (Apple Records, 1970); a desirable seven-inch 45 RPM limited-edition boxed set for the single "When We Was Fab." The double image of George Harrison seen on the cover is by longtime Beatle crony Klaus Voorman, who mimics his own past work from the jacket of the group's REVOLVER in this psychedelic portrait of George (WEA Records, 1988); a rare eight-track for John and Yoko's avant-garde hodge podge UNFINISHED MUSIC NO. 2: LIFE WITH THE LIONS (Zapple Records, 1968); the eight-track cartridge for half of the double album release CONCERT FOR BANGLADESH (Apple Records, 1971); the cassette box for John and Yoko's politically naive SOMETIME IN NEW YORK CITY (Apple Records, 1972); a George Harrison postcard and boxed set containing the single "Got My Mind Set On You" (WEA Records, 1987); a well-turned-out double eight-track package for Yoko Ono's APPROXIMATELY INFINITE UNIVERSE (Apple Records, 1972);* **SECOND ROW** *A limited-edition package for Linda McCartney's reggae inspired "Seaside Woman" released under the pseudonym of Suzy and the Red Stripes. This triple windowed boxed set contains not only the bright yellow single but also an artsy button and a thin pack of so-called "Ten Saucy Postcards" (A & M Records, 1977); an almost antique three and three-quarters IPS monotape of the Beatles, playable only on an early home reel-to-reel tape player (Parlophone Records, 1965); the cassette single for John Lennon's "Woman" (WEA Records, 1981);* **THIRD ROW** *The eight-track tape for John and Yoko's self-indulgent WEDDING ALBUM (Apple Records, 1969); another monotape, this one for A HARD DAY'S NIGHT (Parlophone Records, 1964);* **BOTTOM ROW** *The flip-top cassette single for John's "Watching the Wheels" (WEA Records, 1981) and, finally, another monotape, MEET THE BEATLES (Parlophone Records, 1963).*

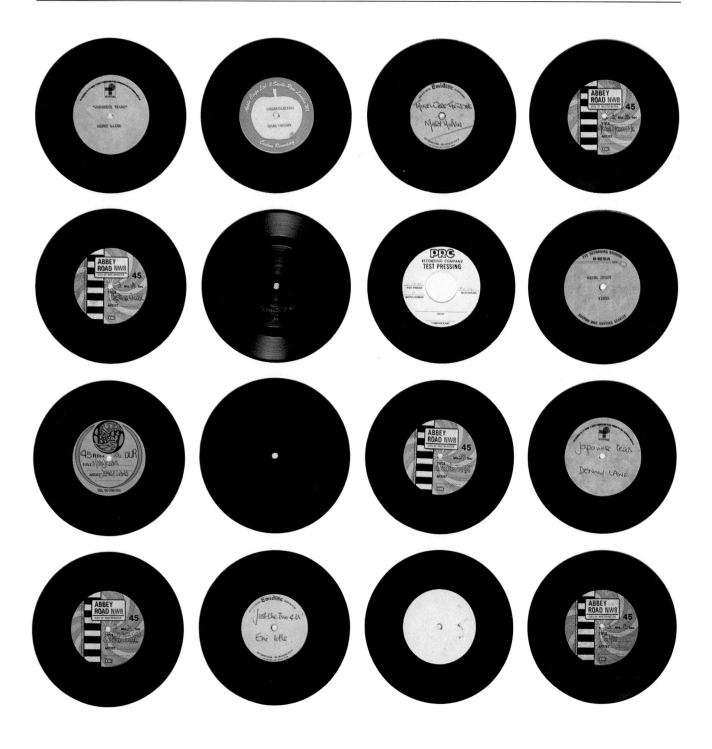

*A grand collection of one-of-a-kind seven-inch acetates:* TOP ROW *"Japanese Tears" by Denny Laine
(Pye Studio); "Congratulations" by Susan Cadigan (Apple Corps Ltd Custom Recording); "Those
Were the Days" by Mary Hopkin (EMI Disc); "Arrow Through Me" (Abbey Road/EMI Studio);*
SECOND ROW *"Getting Closer" (Abbey Road/EMI Studio); no label; PRC Recording Co. Test
Pressing; "Water Spout" by Wings (Pye Recording Studios Custom Disc Cutting Service);* THIRD
ROW *"Moon Dreams" by Denny Laine (Abbey Road/EMI Studio); no label; "We're Open Tonight"
(Abbey Road/EMI Studio); "Japanese Tears" by Denny Laine (Pye Studio);* BOTTOM ROW *A so-called
"cleaner cut" of "Getting Closer" (Abbey Road/EMI Studio); "Just the Two of Us" by Eric Idle
(EMI Disc); no label; "To You" (Abbey Road/EMI Studio).*

ABOVE *Harrison chants the holy name of the Lord Sri Krishna with devotees of the Radha Krishna Temple on the roof of the Beatles' Apple building, 1970;* BELOW *At Abbey Road during sessions for the Apple LP George cut with the mantra-loving followers of Krishna.*

*Ravi Shankar and George Harrison blissed out in the transcendental
sweetness of a quiet Indian grove, 1974.*

*The Harrisons leave Walton-On-Thames Court, after being granted bail on what George still insists was a trumped-up marijuana possession charge, March 19, 1969.*

*The official press photograph released in conjunction with George's 1974 tour;*
**BACKGROUND** *Liverpool, hometown of the Beatles.*

# WATCHING RAINBOWS

## PICTURE DISCS, COLOURED VINYL AND MAXI-SINGLES

The advent of Beatles picture discs in the mid-seventies brought with it an almost rabid desire on the part of hardcore collectors to search out and possess every pressing available. Supplies were often strictly limited and prices skyrocketed in response to the unprecedented and largely unanticipated demand. The initial *Sgt. Pepper* picture disc was issued in America around 1978 at about $15, but was soon selling briskly in the underground market for up to $200. Later, slightly different *Sgt. Pepper* imports began turning up in American record stores, fuelling even more fierce competition among fans to obtain the precious discs. Now, many years later, picture records continue to excite impassioned buyers and are shipped out in vast quantities to retail outlets all over the world.

Other sought-after Beatle-related picture discs manufactured over the years include McCartney's *Band on the Run, Give My Regards*

OPPOSITE PAGE, TOP ROW *The Decca audition tapes issued in yet another form, this time as a double album coloured vinyl/picture disc combo;* SECOND ROW *The open inside gatefold of the LP (Backstage Records, 1982);* BOTTOM ROW *Three picture discs from* SO MUCH YOUNGER THEN, *the visually impressive bootleg boxed set. Musically, the records are inferior, featuring outtakes from various BBC radio sessions already well known to serious Beatles fans (Democratic Records, 1983).*

to *Broadstreet* and the never commercially released picture version of Wings' *Back to the Egg*. The latter is, without doubt, the most valuable of all such records as just two dozen were ever pressed, and then only as special gifts to the band and its production team following the end of recording. In 1989, this author was lucky enough to find one after years of searching and subsequently sold it to a prominent California dealer for $1,800. Several months later, I was shocked to learn that it had been resold at least two more times, finally going for more than $3,000, quite a healthy sum for something that originally was given out free as a souvenir.

John Lennon has had several of his albums issued in picture form as well, *Milk and Honey* and *Walls and Bridges* among them. At least two original Lennon bootleg picture discs have been produced as well. Entitled *Listen to this Picture Record* and the *John Lennon Telecasts*, neither recording was of very high quality and therefore never sold in any great numbers. George Harrison has been the odd man out when it comes to having his music released on picture discs. Only his recent *Cloud Nine* and a seven-inch charity version of his late-seventies single "Faster" have seen the light of day.

Another hot contender for the attention of die-hard Beatle fans is the coloured vinyl recording. Although, like picture discs, coloured vinyl albums have been around for decades, their widespread popularity among consumers wasn't evident until the mid-seventies. Since that time, they have come into their own and are considered by many to be an excellent long-term, virtually risk-free investment for even the most casual Beatle fan. Thanks to these wonderful releases, the Beatles' *"White Album"* may now be purchased in glorious snow-white vinyl, and the psychedelic soundtrack for *Yellow Submarine* truly lives up to its colourful name. Although boasting far better sound quality than picture discs, coloured vinyl isn't really meant to be played either. As with all potentially collectible recordings, the fewer scratches the better. In

fact, I myself have two complete record collections, one I call "playable" and the other, you guessed it, "non-playable."

Probably the most commercially successful of all the many recent innovations in Beatle collectibles is the twelve-inch maxi-single. A hold-over from the North American disco craze of the silly seventies, these oversized singles afforded the listener a chance to enjoy the "feel" of old-time 45s coupled with the overall convenience and presence of an album. Graphically, maxi-singles offer considerable high quality, original Beatle-related art work, with celebrated designers on both sides of the Atlantic providing a glorious array of appealing covers.

Of the former Beatles, it is Paul McCartney who seems to be the most taken with these super-singles, personally overseeing the design and production of numerous such releases. Since his death, John's music has also entered the maxi market in a big way, with only George and Ringo lagging behind in cashing in on the popular and lucrative releases. Happily for serious fans maxis, too, offer excellent potential as Beatle collectibles, given their somewhat limited-edition status, crisp sound and bold, original designs. Already the promotion-only Lennon releases for "Starting Over" and "Watching the Wheels" are fetching big bucks (around $100) at record conventions, as are several of Paul's early musical efforts with Wings, such as the disco-inspired "Goodnight Tonight" and the manic "Temporary Secretary."

All things considered, these days the unbeatable trio of Beatle-oriented picture discs, coloured vinyl albums and maxi-singles represent virtually the only way "in" for young collectors desirous of ever possessing a reasonably priced Beatles library. Begin buying now for tomorrow is about the best advice possible for any lingering "late bloomers" just starting out. If you pick and choose carefully, the $10 or $20 record you grab now could be worth relatively big money in just a few short years.

*One of the most bizarre Beatle-related records ever:* TOP *a Russian combination flexi/picture disc for John's touching "Watching the Wheels" (no information available);* BOTTOM *The front cover.*

*Beatle picture discs:* **TOP ROW** *The obscure German issue of* SGT. PEPPER *(no information available);* TIMELESS II *(Silhouette Records, 1982);* TIMELESS *(Silhouette Records, 1981);* **SECOND ROW** THE SILVER BEATLES *(Ultra Sound Records, 1982);* BEATLES TRACKS FROM SANTA CLAUS *(no information available); Unknown (no information available);* **BOTTOM ROW** *A disc from* SO MUCH YOUNGER THEN *(Democratic Records, 1983); Unknown (no information available), and finally* ABBEY ROAD *(Capitol Records, 1978).*

*A collection of Beatle-related picture discs:* **TOP ROW** *A special die-cut 45 for Paul McCartney's noisy "Spies Like Us" (Parlophone Records, 1985); a twelve-inch single for the same tune (Parlophone Records, 1985); an appealing cut-out for the children's song "We All Stand Together" from the MPL-produced animated short* RUPERT THE BEAR AND THE FROG SONG *(Parlophone Records, 1984);* **SECOND ROW** *The B side to the coveted* SGT. PEPPER *picture disc (Capitol Records, 1978); another disc from the 1983 bootleg set* SO MUCH YOUNGER THEN *(Democratic Records, 1983); a bootleg picture disc for the heralded* CHRISTMAS ALBUM *(no information available);* **BOTTOM ROW** *The Beatles' "A Hard Day's Night" (EMI Records, 1984); an octagonal-shaped picture disc for "Beatle Rap" by the Qworymen (Erika Records, 1982), and the single for "I Feel Fine" (EMI Records, 1984).*

TOP ROW *Paul McCartney picture disc B sides:* NO MORE LONELY NIGHTS *(Parlophone Records, 1984) and* BAND ON THE RUN *(Capitol Records, 1978);* SECOND ROW *The uninspired picture record for the* JOHN LENNON TELECASTS *bootleg (no information available); John and Yoko's* MILK AND HONEY *(Polygram Records, 1984), and* (BOTTOM) *the clever* LISTEN TO THIS PICTURE RECORD *(no information available), an interesting Lennon interview bootleg.*

**TOP ROW** *Just to prove there is nothing new under the sun, an early flexi-disc from the late forties and a stylish picture record from the Second World War;* **BOTTOM ROW, LEFT** *Trading today at just over $50, this seven-inch Julian Lennon picture disc is highly prized by collectors;* **RIGHT** *Collectors snapped up virtually every copy of this "Valotte" picture disc upon its release in 1984. After a two-year search the author finally located this copy in a record store on the remote island of Guernsey, between England and France.*

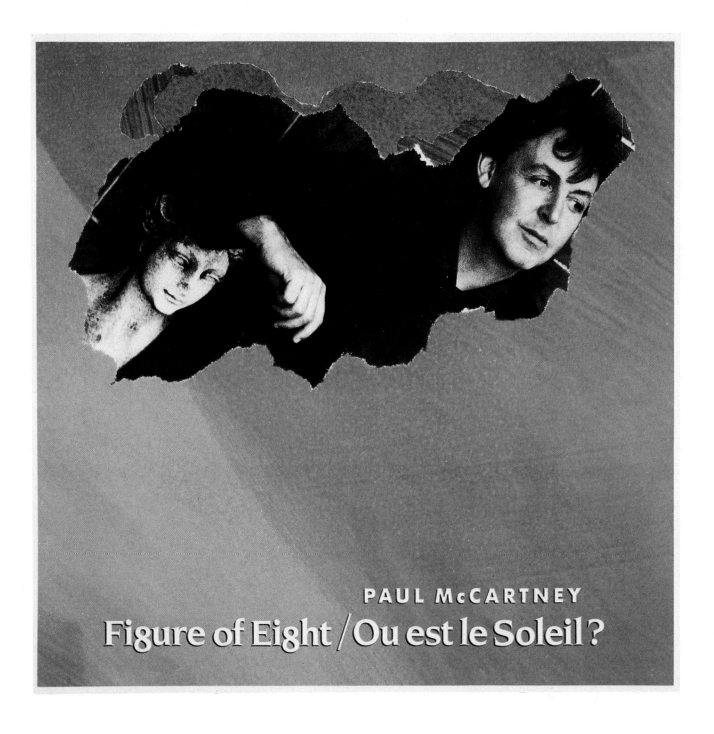

*A twelve-inch maxi-single for McCartney's bouncy "Figure of Eight" and soulful
"Ou est le Soleil?" as released in Belgium (Parlophone Records, 1989).*

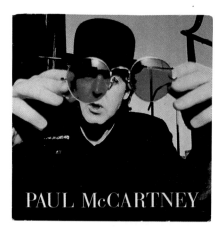
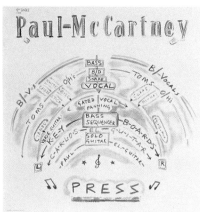

*Paul McCartney-related maxi singles:* TOP ROW *"Seaside Woman"and "Suzy and the Red Stripes"*
*(EMI Records, 1977); "Pretty Little Head" (EMI Records, 1986); "My Brave Face" (Parlophone*
*Records, 1989);* SECOND ROW *"Press" (Capitol Records, 1986); "Only Love Remains" (EMI Records,*
*1986); "Spies Like Us" (EMI Records, 1985);* BOTTOM ROW *"Take it Away" (Columbia Records,*
*1982); "Ebony and Ivory" with Stevie Wonder (Columbia Records, 1982).*

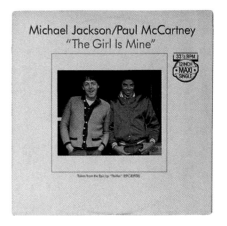

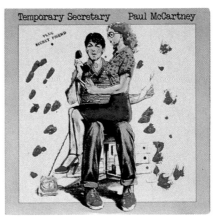

*Paul McCartney maxi singles:* **TOP ROW** *"Goodnight Tonight," autographed by Denny Laine
(Columbia Records, 1979); "No More Lonely Nights" (EMI Records, 1984); "Ou est le Soleil?"
(EMI Records, 1989);* **SECOND ROW** *"Once Upon a Long Ago" (EMI Records, 1987); "This One"
(EMI Records, 1989); "The Girl is Mine" with Michael Jackson (Epic Records, 1982);* **BOTTOM ROW**
*"Say Say Say" with Michael Jackson (Columbia Records, 1983); "Temporary Secretary"
(EMI Records, 1980).*

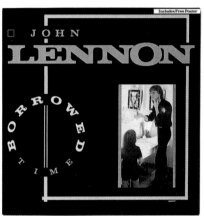

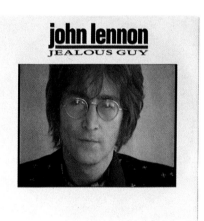

*John and Yoko maxi-singles:* **TOP ROW** *"Nobody Told Me" (Polygram Records, 1983); "Give Peace a Chance" (Apple Records, 1969); "I Saw Her Standing There" with Elton John and the Muscle Shoals Horns (DJM Records, 1981);* **SECOND ROW** *"Borrowed Time" (Polygram Records, 1984); "Never Say Goodbye" (Polygram Records, 1983); "Borrowed Time" (Polygram Records, 1984);* **BOTTOM ROW** *"Imagine" (Apple Records, 1975); "Jealous Guy" (EMI Records, 1985).*

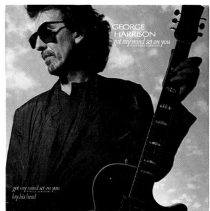

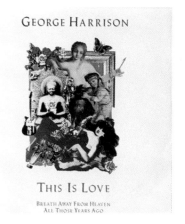
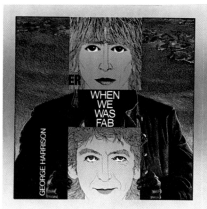

OPPOSITE PAGE *John and Yoko maxi-singles:* TOP ROW *"Imagine" (Apple Records, 1971);*
*"I'm Stepping Out" (Polygram Records, 1984);* SECOND ROW *"Walking on Thin Ice" (Geffen*
*Records, 1981); "Whatever Gets You Thru the Night" with Elton John and the Muscle Shoals Horns*
*(DJM Records, 1975);* BOTTOM ROW *"(Just Like) Starting Over" (Geffen Records, 1980); "No No No"*
*(Geffen Records, 1981);* ABOVE *Samples of the few George Harrison-related twelve-inch singles issued*
*over the last few years:* TOP ROW *"Got My Mind Set On You" with generic cover (Dark Horse*
*Records, 1987); "Got My Mind Set On You" (Dark Horse Records, 1987);* BOTTOM ROW *"This is*
*Love" (WEA Records, 1988); "When We Was Fab" (WEA Records, 1988); The Traveling Wilburys'*
*"Handle With Care" (Warner/Wilbury Records, 1988).*

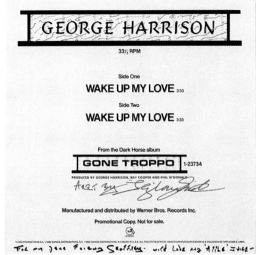

*Although the general public may not realize it, many of their favourite records were first issued in white cardboard-covered, DJ-only promotional packages. A few Beatle-related examples:* **TOP ROW** *"All Those Years Ago" (Dark Horse Records, 1981); "Wake Up My Love" autographed by "Legs" Larry Smith (Dark Horse Records, 1982);* **SECOND ROW** *"Happy Xmas (War is Over)" (Geffen Records, 1982); "WEA Sampler" featuring John Lennon's "Starting Over" (WEA Records, 1980);* **BOTTOM ROW** *"A Personal Music Dialogue with George Harrison" (Dark Horse Records, 1976); Suzy and the Red Stripes' (alias Linda McCartney and Wings) "Seaside Woman" (Epic Records, 1977).*

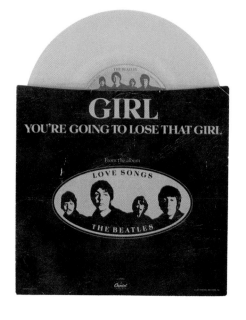

*Much sought-after coloured vinyl for the albums* (TOP ROW) *LET IT BE (Apple Records, 1970) and*
(SECOND ROW) *the ill-conceived REEL MUSIC (Capitol Records, 1982);* BOTTOM LEFT *Perhaps the
rarest coloured single of them all, a DJ-only copy of the song "Girl," complete with a tooled leather-
look picture sleeve and golden disc (Capitol Records, 1977).*

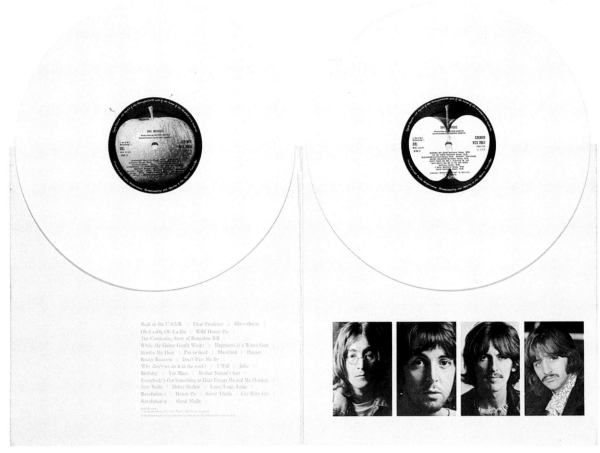

**ABOVE** *The "WHITE ALBUM" as you always wanted to see it, in deluxe all-white vinyl (Apple Records, 1968);* **BELOW** *The Beatles' schmaltzy compilation* LOVE SONGS *in valuable limited-edition gold, with an inside gatefold photo by Richard Avedon (Capitol Records, 1977).*

*The stylish double-disc/two-volume "greatest hits" compilation:* **TOP ROW** THE BEATLES/1967–1970
*in blue vinyl and* **(BOTTOM ROW)** THE BEATLES/1962–1966 *in flaming red (Apple Records, 1973).*

**TOP AND SECOND ROW** *Bootleg seven-inch singles culled from the now historic Decca audition tapes for an added bit of public appeal, issued here in coloured vinyl (Deccagone Records, date unknown);* **BOTTOM** *Performing "Hey Jude" on "The David Frost Show," London, 1968.*

**TOP ROW** *An in-house record company promotion billed as A SAMPLER FROM TUG OF WAR issued in white (Columbia Records, 1982);* **BELOW** *The McCartney Productions Limited (MPL) token reggae act The Cimarons' twelve-inch single released as a combination picture disc/coloured vinyl record (1982).*

**TOP ROW** *John and Yoko's "Happy Xmas (War is Over)" sporting the official label (Apple Records, 1971); "Sisters, O Sisters," B side of John and Yoko's "Woman is the Nigger of the World" (Apple Records, 1972); "Listen, the Snow is Falling," B side of John and Yoko's "Happy Xmas (War is Over)" (Apple Records, 1971);* **BOTTOM ROW** *A limited-edition industry promotional twelve-inch single of "Happy Xmas (War is Over)," issued on white vinyl (Capitol Records, 1986); a Japanese issue of John Lennon's first "greatest hits" package,* SHAVED FISH, *pressed on green vinyl (EMI Records, 1975).*

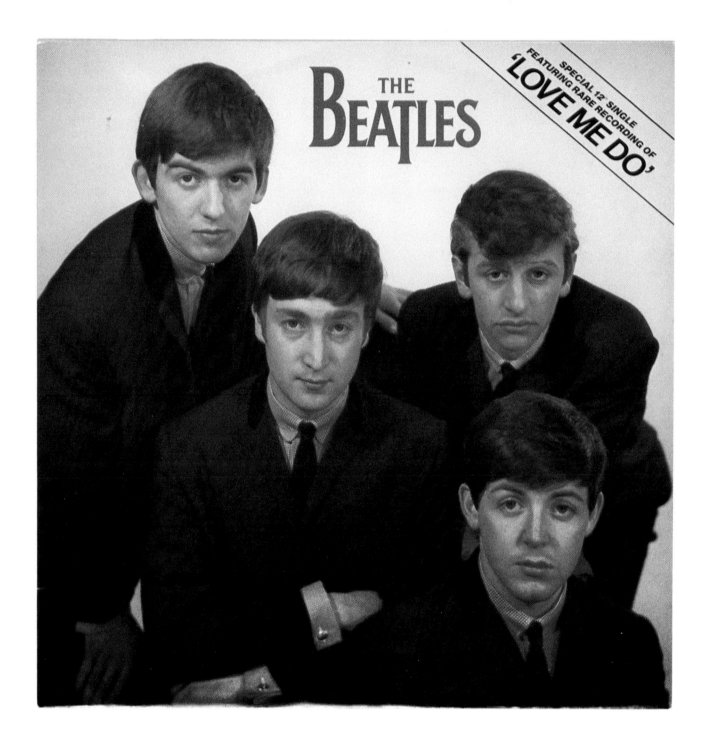

*The maxi-single for the Beatles' "Love Me Do" reissued yet again in the late eighties.*

ABOVE *Ringo Starr in an early seventies promo pic;* BELOW *Sir Richard Attenborough, Peter Sellers and Ringo say "cheese" during the filming of* THE MAGIC CHRISTIAN *at Pinewood Studios, London, 1969;* OPPOSITE PAGE *Ringo takes off in his role as Youngman Grand in* THE MAGIC CHRISTIAN.

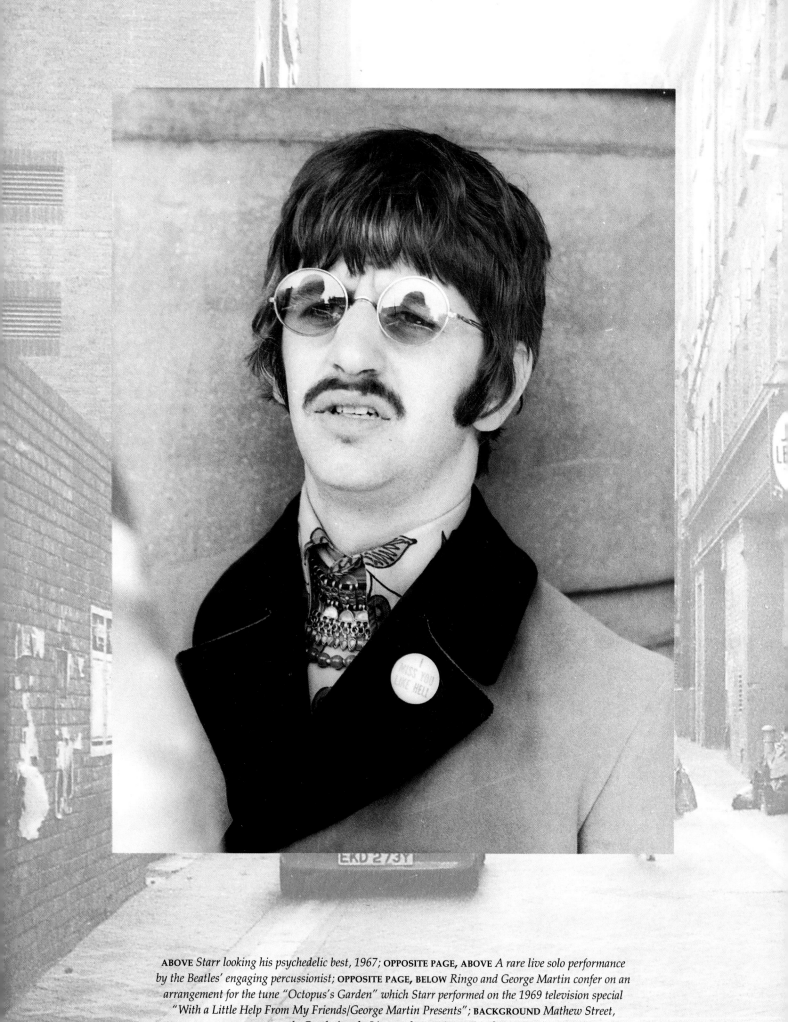

ABOVE *Starr looking his psychedelic best, 1967*; OPPOSITE PAGE, ABOVE *A rare live solo performance by the Beatles' engaging percussionist*; OPPOSITE PAGE, BELOW *Ringo and George Martin confer on an arrangement for the tune "Octopus's Garden" which Starr performed on the 1969 television special "With a Little Help From My Friends/George Martin Presents"*; BACKGROUND *Mathew Street, the Beatles' early Liverpool stomping ground.*

# 7

# LOOKING GLASS

## APPLE RECORDS LTD

Today virtually everything anybody ever wanted to know about the Beatles' Apple Corp Ltd has already been written, broadcast, documented and re-written at least a thousand times. One rather obvious angle, however – the ambitious music released by the company – has until now received little attention from the faithful.

Most people are aware that the great green Granny Smith Apple label hosted several groups other then its four illustrious founders, but do they realize just how many? Are people aware of the exceedingly wide range of music Apple sponsored and subsequently produced? How about such rare and obscure releases as quasi-classical composer John Tavener's *Celtic Requiem,* Badfinger's first-incarnation album *Maybe Tomorrow* released under the name of the Iveys, or even the mantra-mad Radha Krishna Temple's Apple LP produced by Beatle George?

Established in April, 1968, "Apple was a manifestation of Beatle naïvety," John Lennon remarked in the mid-seventies. "We were going to try and help everybody, but we were conned on both the subtlest and bluntest levels. We really didn't get approached by the

*The original promotional poster for the popular 1970
"Govinda" single from the devotees of Sri Krishna.*

best artists. We had to quickly build up a wall to protect ourselves from all the beggars and lepers in Britain and America who came to see us. Our lives were getting insane! I tried to see everyone day-in, day-out, but there really wasn't anyone who had much to offer society or to me . . . Once you open the door, it's very hard, you know."

On top of the tidal wave of talent and lack of talent heaped upon the fledgling concern there were other, bigger problems as well. After losing money consistently, New York show business big-shot Allen Klein was brought in by John, George and Ringo to help straighten things out – much to the chagrin of Paul, who was keen on his father-in-law, attorney Lee Eastman, taking control.

"Klein had done a good job with the Rolling Stones previously," remembers Lennon confidant and Apple insider Ritchie Yorke, "wrangling an impressive raise in their record royalties as well as helping streamline their often faltering collective fortunes. John, for one, was impressed by his salt-of-the-earth personality and straightforward, bottom-line approach to business." Paul, however, remained steadfastly unconvinced of both Klein's management abilities and his honesty. He therefore stubbornly held out his slice of the Apple pie for the Eastmans to handle.

At one point, the feud reached such ridiculous proportions that McCartney instructed Apple staff to obscure Klein's company name (ABKCO) and address from promotional copies of the *Let It Be* album by manually sticking small pieces of black tape over it. To make matters worse, Brian Epstein's brother Clive – who now controlled Nemperor Holdings, his family's interest in the Beatles – sold 70 percent of its shares to the powerful Triumph Investment Trust. Even more upsetting to the Beatles' precarious Apple cart was the sale of Nemperor's share of Northern

Songs, the Beatles' original music publisher, to Sir Lew Grade's Associated Television Corporation for a princely sum. This was the last straw. Now it seemed the boys would forever be singing only for a boardroom of tired business suits, where the only real concern was figuring out just what to do with the millions of pounds generated by the Beatles' own souped-up brand of rock 'n' roll.

Despite Apple's many management difficulties, the music issued by the label very often triumphed over the madness. Artists like the talented Welsh songbird Mary Hopkin, the hard-rocking Badfinger, the bitter-sweet James Taylor and the soulful Billy Preston ultimately lent considerable credibility to the rookie label, not to mention the highly esteemed presence of the Fab Four at the top of the company's artist roster.

In a 1984 interview at her home in Shiplake, Oxfordshire, Mary Hopkin shared some of her thoughts on the label. "I think it was a lovely concept. Very typical of the sixties to have this wonderful idea of one big family and giving everybody an opportunity to be a success. But it attracts all the hangers-on, you see. I think they [the Beatles] realized that after a while, unfortunately after a lot of money had already been spent and gone down the drain."

Apple tried hard to live up to the high-flown ideals on which it was founded, but unfortunately bottomed out badly when squared off against the harsh realities of the "pounds, shillings and pence" mentality of the mainstream music business.

Still, in its heyday, the little label that tried to touch the sky managed to give the world some magical moments, from the shimmering Indian ragas of Ravi Shankar to the cool jazz of the Modern Jazz Quartet, from the socio-political buffoonery of left-wing radical David Peel to the unforgettable melodies of the Beatles themselves.

*Apple albums from the popular band Badfinger (formerly the Iveys):* **FIRST COLUMN, TOP TO BOTTOM**
*MAYBE TOMORROW and the back cover (1969);* **SECOND COLUMN** *The open outside gatefold to NO
DICE (1970); ASS (1973);* **THIRD COLUMN** *MAGIC CHRISTIAN MUSIC (1970); STRAIGHT UP (1971).*

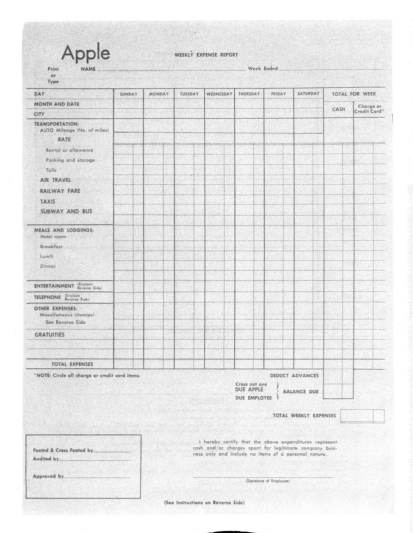

**APPLE**
54 St. James's Street
London SW1

telephone 01-629 8222

### GENESIS CHAPTER 2

21 And the LORD God caused a
deep sleep to fall upon Adam,
and he slept: and he took one of
his ribs, and closed up the flesh
instead thereof;
22 And the rib, which the LORD
God had taken from man, made
he a woman, and brought her
unto the man.
23 And Adam said, This *is* now
bone of my bones, and flesh of
my flesh: she shall be called
Woman, because she was taken
out of Man.
24 Therefore shall a man leave
his father and his mother, and
shall cleave unto his wife: and
they shall be one flesh.

**25 And they were both naked,
the man and his wife, and were
not ashamed.**

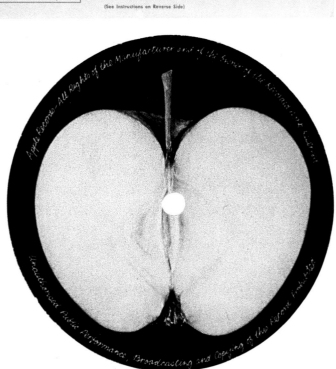

TOP LEFT *After tough New York rock magnate Allen Klein took control of Apple in 1969, things
tightened up considerably as this meticulous expense report attests:* TOP RIGHT *An original Apple
calling card valued today at over $100;* RIGHT *A classy promotional hand–out conceived by publicist
Derek Taylor for John and Yoko's* TWO VIRGINS; BOTTOM LEFT *The famous B side of the famous Apple.*

TOP LEFT *The original Apple ad seeking new music artists which caused an avalanche of audition tapes, promotional glossies and resumés to pour into the Beatles' Baker Street offices;* TOP RIGHT *An advert for the short-lived Apple Studios located in the basement of the Beatles' plush Savile Row headquarters;* BOTTOM *The Apple we've known for all these years as it appeared in an insert for George Harrison's eclectic* WONDERWALL *LP.*

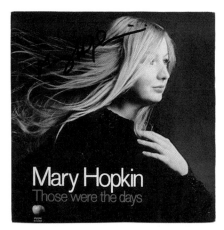

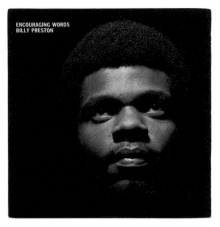

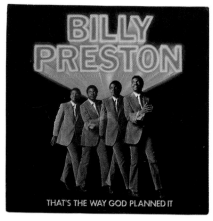
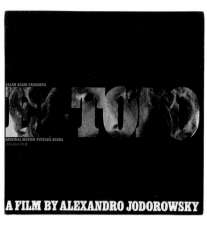

*Apple LPs:* **TOP ROW** *Three Mary Hopkin albums autographed by the artist:* THOSE WERE THE DAYS *(1972);* EARTH SONG *(1971);* POSTCARD *(1969);* **SECOND ROW** *Billy Preston,* ENCOURAGING WORDS *(1970); the sound track for the film* COME TOGETHER *(1971); The Modern Jazz Quartet,* UNDER THE JASMIN TREE *(1968);* **BOTTOM ROW** *Billy Preston,* THAT'S THE WAY GOD PLANNED IT *(1969); the sound track from the film* EL TOPO *(1971); The Modern Jazz Quartet,* SPACE *(1969).*

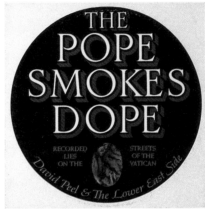

*Apple LPs:* **TOP ROW** *Jackie Lomax,* IS THIS WHAT YOU WANT? *(1969); Elephant's Memory,*
ELEPHANT'S MEMORY *(1972); James Taylor,* JAMES TAYLOR *(1968);* **SECOND ROW** *Doris Troy,*
DORIS TROY *(1970); David Peel,* THE POPE SMOKES DOPE *(1972); Lon and Derrek Van Eaton,*
BROTHER *(1972);* **BOTTOM** *Phil Spector,* PHIL SPECTOR'S CHRISTMAS ALBUM *(1972).*

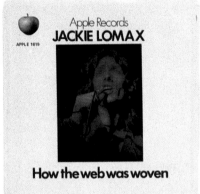

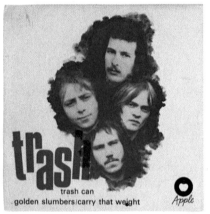

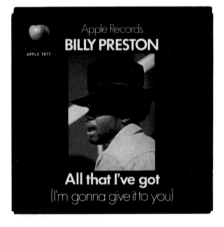

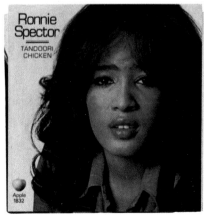

*A rare collection of Apple single sleeves:* **OPPOSITE PAGE, TOP ROW** *Jackie Lomax, "How the Web was Woven"; Jackie Lomax "How the Web was Woven"; Jackie Lomax, "Sour Milk Sea";* **SECOND ROW** *The Iveys, "Maybe Tomorrow"; Badfinger, "Baby Blue"; Trash, "Trash Can";* **THIRD ROW** *Trash, "Road To Nowhere"; Billy Preston, "That's the Way God Planned it"; Billy Preston, "All That I've Got";* **BOTTOM ROW** *Ronnie Spector, "Tandoori Chicken"; Mary Hopkin, "San Remo '69"; Five from Mary Hopkin:* **ABOVE, TOP ROW** *"Temma Harbour"; "Que Sera, Sera"; "Think About Your Children";* **SECOND ROW** *"Water, Paper and Clay"; "A Song for Europe"; Lon and Derrek Van Eaton, "Sweet Music";* **BOTTOM ROW** *Elephant's Memory Band, "Liberation Special"; Chris Hodge, "We're On Our Way"; Elastic Oz Band, "God Save Us."*

*For serious Apple collectors the more obscure the material, the better. Memorabilia relating to Apple's RADHA KRISHNA TEMPLE LP;* **LEFT COLUMN** *Three rare 45 picture sleeves and* (**TOP RIGHT**) *a valuable poster announcing the transcendental release;* **OPPOSITE PAGE** *The many faces of Apple. Over the years the company's Gene Mahon-designed logo evolved significantly in both colour and cut. A few examples as seen on the singles:* **TOP ROW** *The Beatles' "Let it Be" (1970); Ringo's "Back Off Boogaloo" (1972); The Beatles' "Let it Be" (1970);* **SECOND ROW** *Yoko Ono's "Move On Fast" (1972); The Beatles' "All You Need is Love" (1967);* **BELOW** *Original artifacts:* **TOP ROW** *An Apple postcard; a three-dimensional Apple Mobile cube sent out to members of the Beatle Fan Club and an Apple shipping box for singles;* **SECOND ROW** *A very rare bit of Apple history, the official 1971 fold-out Christmas tree ornament;* **THIRD ROW** *A pristine Apple single mailer, autographed by Beatle bigwig Derek Taylor; another Apple postcard, this time with a specially commissioned logo by artist Alan Aldridge; an unused label for the Mary Hopkin album POSTCARD; a pack of genuine Apple matches (circa 1969) and a one-of-a-kind brass apple presented to John Lennon by the Apple office staff in 1970.*

*Apple LPs:* **TOP ROW** *John Tavener,* THE WHALE *(1970);* CELTIC REQUIEM *(1971), perhaps the most difficult-to-find Apple LP ever;* **BOTTOM ROW** *Official "The Pope Smokes Dope" rolling papers, issued as a naughty promotional give-away for David Peel and the Lower East Side by Apple Records; a rare poster by Frank Poole promoting a concert by eccentric Apple artist David Peel.*

SUNDOWN PLAYBOYS

 Apple Records - 1700 Broadway, New York, N.Y.

TOP RIGHT *Apple's Hot Chocolate Band takes a stab at covering the Plastic Ono Band's "Give Peace a Chance" (1969) and* (TOP LEFT) *the B side to the now highly collectible and valuable Sundown Playboys' "Saturday Nite Special" released on 78 RPM (1972);* BELOW *Sundown Playboys promo pic.*

Apple Records **PLASTIC ONO BAND** 3 Savile Row, London W1

Apple Records **THE BEATLES** 3 Savile Row, London W1

Apple Records 3 Savile Row, London W1

**GEORGE HARRISON**

Apple Records

Distributed by Capitol Records, Inc.

## THE BEATLES

Apple Records

Distributed by Capitol Records Distributing Corp.

## THE BEATLES

Apple Records

Distributed by Capitol Records Distributing Corp.

OPPOSITE PAGE AND ABOVE *Official Apple Records promotional photographs.*

**OPPOSITE PAGE, ABOVE** *Winter fun during filming for the Beatles' second feature film* HELP!;
**OPPOSITE PAGE, BELOW** *Three-part harmony at Abbey Road, 1963;* **ABOVE** *Kicking up their heels on British television, 1965.*

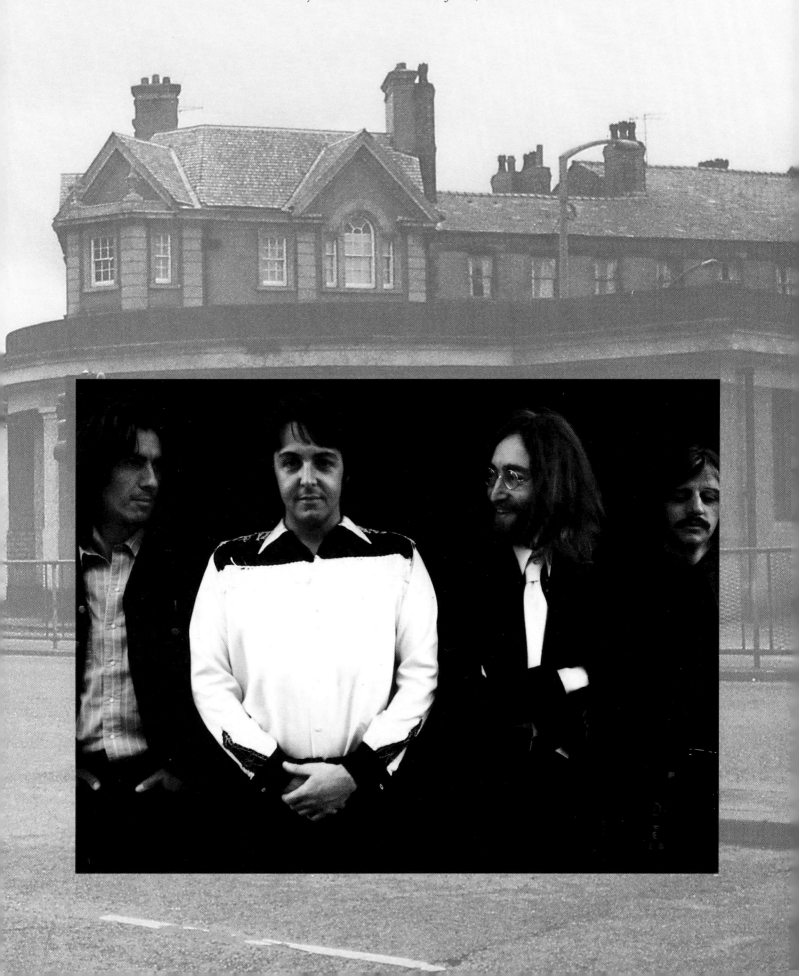

OPPOSITE PAGE, ABOVE *The Beatles at the official press reception for* SGT. PEPPER'S LONELY HEARTS CLUB BAND, *held at manager Brian Epstein's opulent Belgravia townhouse in Chapel Street, 1967;* OPPOSITE PAGE, BELOW *International advocates of the philosophy of love, peace and light, 1967;* BELOW *Four Beatles, four different moods, 1969;* BACKGROUND *The suburban Liverpool roundabout made famous in the Beatles' "Penny Lane," 1967.*

# 8

# I SHOULD LIKE TO LIVE UP A TREE

## BEATLE-RELATED RECORDINGS

Throughout the Beatles' long and celebrated collective and solo careers they often became involved either in performing on, composing for, or producing other people's records. Artists as diverse as Alvin Lee, Johnny Winter, Paul Simon, Keith Moon, Billy J. Kramer, Denny Laine, the Rolling Stones, Cilla Black, Eric Clapton, David Bowie, Elton John, Harry Nilsson and Peggy Lee have all worked with the Beatles in various capacities and combinations. Blood, however, is thicker than water and the Beatles were no exception. Over the years, all the boys pitched in their considerable talents to work with, or at least actively encourage and oversee, the fledgling careers of various family members. Paul, for instance, has laboured long and hard over the years to help his younger brother Mike McGear become a successful entertainer, both with his group the Scaffold and on his own. Whether producing, arranging, composing or performing, Paul's input into Mike's career has been pivotal. McCartney's initial creative involvement with his multi-talented sibling began with his production of the album *McGough & McGear* for Parlophone Records (first released

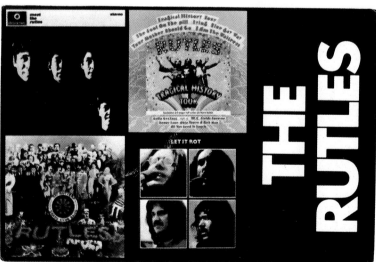

**ABOVE** *An obscure Rutles single from Great Britain, "I Must Be in Love." The boys are, left to right,
Dirk (Eric Idle, of Monty Python fame), Stig (Rikki Fataar), Nasty (Neil Innes, formerly with the
Bonzo Dog Doo Dah Band) and (seated) Barry (John Halsey) (Warner Bros. Records, 1978);*
**BELOW** *A rare postcard issued to promote the popular 1978 NBC television parody "The Rutles."*

in Great Britain on May 17, 1968).

From there, Paul went on to produce the Scaffold's hit single "Liverpool Lou," as well as the superlative solo album *McGear* in 1974 for which he wrote two tunes and co-wrote another seven with brother Mike. Featuring Wings cohorts Denny Laine, drummer Denny Seiwell, guitarist Jimmy McCulloch, and wife Linda, the album *McGear* was nothing less than a first-class Wings album with Mike as guest vocalist. Despite such herculean efforts, however, McGear's career as a pop singer began to wane significantly by the mid-seventies. Eventually Mike took on a new vocation as an author and photographer of some renown.

Another McCartney family member, cousin Kate Robbins, has also benefited from Paul's professional expertise. A crackerjack musical all-rounder back home in Great Britain, Kate was lucky enough to persuade McCartney to produce her rendition of the song "Tomorrow" from the popular Broadway musical *Annie*. Interestingly, the rights to the song just happened to be held by Paul's London-based music-publishing firm MPL. Issued in England on the Anchor label on June 30, 1978, the single didn't quite catch fire with record buyers and soon disappeared. Robbins, however, did go on to host a popular television variety show with her brother and has since scored several hit records on her own.

John Lennon almost certainly envisioned both his sons entering the business at some level. Not surprisingly, eldest offspring Julian Lennon waited only until his twentieth birthday before jumping in with both feet with the moving debut album *Valotte*. It spawned not just one but three popular singles: "Valotte," "Too Late For Goodbyes" and the plaintive anti-drug ballad "Jesse."

Admirably overcoming the comparisons to his famous father's low-pitched tenor, Julian was able to step out from John's giant shadow to become an interesting artist in his own right. Although his two subsequent albums *The Secret Value Of Daydreaming* and *Mr. Jordan* weren't up to the high standard of

*Valotte*, the young Lennon, I believe, still has plenty of memorable music tucked away inside and will continue to successfully sidestep the pitfalls that must come from the incredible pressure generated by his blue-blood rock 'n' roll lineage.

Ringo, too, has invested considerable energy in helping his eldest offspring, Zak, establish a name for himself as a top pop drummer in his own right. Surprisingly, it was the Who's manic percussionist Keith Moon who originally inspired Zak to pick up the sticks, and not his legendary dad. Now that Zak is an adult, however, the old man has generously offered his eldest a helping hand. He hired Zak as one of several sidemen on his 1990 American tour, and joined his son in the video for guitarist Little Stevie's controversial 1985 anti-apartheid single "I Ain't Gonna Play Sun City."

George, too, has faithfully supported two of his brother's children in their aspirations for a behind-the-scenes career in the business by steadfastly offering both his moral and financial assistance.

Since the Beatles first exploded on an unsuspecting world three decades ago, countless Beatle-related records have made their way onto the charts, each struggling to find a place for themselves by aligning their sound and image with that of the Fab Four. On a few occasions, these results were genuinely inspiring, as with Mike McGear's "Man Who Found God on the Moon," Denny Laine's McCartney-penned and -produced "The Note You Never Wrote" and Peter and Gordon's touching interpretation of the Lennon/McCartney ballad "World Without Love." But generally it took the finely honed talents of the Beatles themselves to really "fill out" their compositions with the required charisma and subtlety, a hallmark of their great work.

Although the collectibility of some Beatle-related releases may be negligible, many are fun and tend to illustrate the zaniness that was Beatlemania. Great artists aside, an act like the all-girl Beatle Buddies, the Chipmunks or the terminally preppy Brothers Four croaking out their imitations of the great music of Lennon and McCartney does make you wonder! An even greater testament to the absolute power of the Beatles was that, with few exceptions, most of these blatantly bizarre rip-off albums generally sold extremely well.

ABOVE *Beatles spoof band, The Rutles, autographed by band leader "Nasty" (Neil Innes);* BELOW *The Paul McCartney-produced 1968 hit for the satirical and ingenious Bonzo Dog Doo Dah Band's "I'm the Urban Spaceman." Note: the record company must have been asleep at the wheel when this picture cover was produced as the tune is incorrectly titled "I'm the Urban Spacemen" (Liberty Records, 1968).*

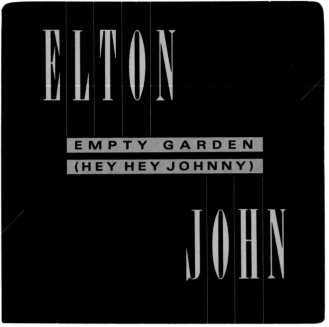

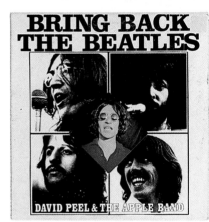

TOP ROW *Keith Moon says "Hi, y'all" on the cover of his one and only, off-the-wall solo LP featuring the John Lennon tune "Move Over Mrs L." (MCA Records, 1975); Elton John's ode to his fallen friend and colleague John Lennon, "Empty Garden (Hey Hey Johnny)" (Geffen Records, 1982);* SECOND ROW *Three typically outrageous recordings from latter-day Apple artist and musical revolutionary David Peel:* BRING BACK THE BEATLES *(Orange Records, 1977);* HAVE A MARIJUANA *(Elektra Records, 1968); and finally* THE AMERICAN REVOLUTION *(Elektra Records, 1970);* OPPOSITE PAGE *Memorabilia relating to the sixties combo Billy J. Kramer with the Dakotas managed by Brian Epstein:* (ABOVE) *the programme from one of their manic shows, and* (RIGHT) *the obscure cover to one of the group's early press kits.*

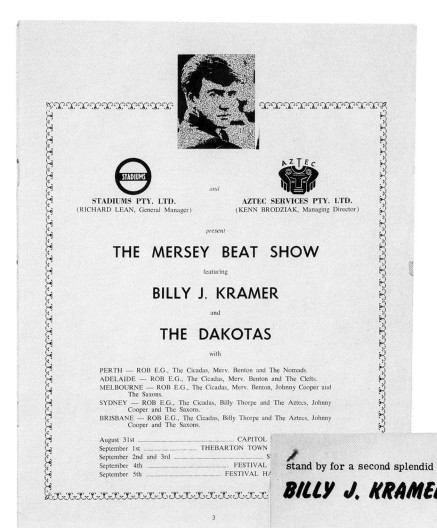

STADIUMS PTY. LTD.
(RICHARD LEAN, General Manager)

*and*

AZTEC SERVICES PTY. LTD.
(KENN BRODZIAK, Managing Director)

*present*

# THE MERSEY BEAT SHOW

*featuring*

## BILLY J. KRAMER

*and*

## THE DAKOTAS

*with*

PERTH — ROB E.G., The Cicadas, Merv. Benton and The Nomads.
ADELAIDE — ROB E.G., The Cicadas, Merv. Benton and The Clefts.
MELBOURNE — ROB E.G., The Cicadas, Merv. Benton, Johnny Cooper and The Saxons.
SYDNEY — ROB E.G., The Cicadas, Billy Thorpe and The Aztecs, Johnny Cooper and The Saxons.
BRISBANE — ROB E.G., The Cicadas, Billy Thorpe and The Aztecs, Johnny Cooper and The Saxons.

| | | |
|---|---|---|
| August 31st | .................... | CAPITOL |
| September 1st | .................... | THEBARTON TOWN |
| September 2nd and 3rd | .................... | S |
| September 4th | .................... | FESTIVAL |
| September 5th | .................... | FESTIVAL H/ |

3

stand by for a second splendid single from

## BILLY J. KRAMER WITH THE DAKOTAS

billy's    beatle - penned    ballad
"bad  to  me"  should  become  his
second  consecutive  chart-topper!

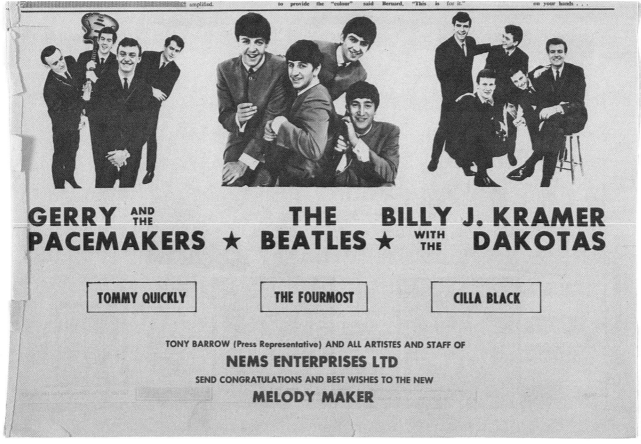

ABOVE *A preppy looking Billy J. on a collectible picture cover for "I'll Keep You Satisfied" (Imperial Records, 1964). By the way, the "J" was awarded to Kramer, whose real name was William Ashton, by John Lennon who said it stood for "Jesus";* BELOW *Christmas greetings from NEMS enterprises to the heralded British music business rag* MELODY MAKER.

THE
DAKOTAS
WITH
PETE MACLAINE

THE DIXON AGENCY,
45 LLOYD STREET,
MANCHESTER, 2.
BLA 6363

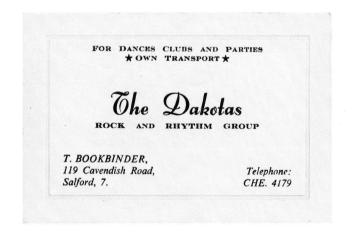

FOR DANCES CLUBS AND PARTIES
★ OWN TRANSPORT ★

*The Dakotas*
ROCK AND RHYTHM GROUP

T. BOOKBINDER,
119 Cavendish Road,
Salford, 7.

Telephone:
CHE. 4179

ABOVE *The Dakotas first publicity photo while singer Pete MacLaine was still fronting the group;* BELOW *An original calling card for the band.*

 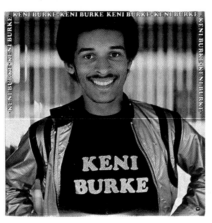 

*Dark Horse Records, George Harrison's personal record label formed in 1974:* **TOP ROW** *Splinter,
TWO MAN BAND (1977); Splinter, THE PLACE I LOVE (1974); Splinter, HARDER TO LIVE (1975);*
**SECOND ROW** *Attitudes, GOOD NEWS (1977); Attitudes, ATTITUDES (1976); Henry McCullough,
MIND YOUR OWN BUSINESS! (1975);* **BOTTOM ROW** *Stairsteps, 2ND RESURRECTION (1975);
Keni Burke, KENI BURKE (1977); Jiva, JIVA (1975).*

*Music by Paul's baby brother, Mike McGear:* **TOP ROW** *The obscure* WOMAN *(Island Records, 1972);*
**SECOND ROW** *The open inside gatefold for Mike's brilliant* McGEAR *(Warner Bros. Records, 1974);*
**BOTTOM ROW** *The front cover to* McGEAR; *See For Miles Records' release of the Scaffold's* SINGLES A'S
*& B's, a nifty compilation showcasing the very best of this legendary tribe of musical fools (1982).*

*Beatle-related Indian spiritual albums:* **TOP ROW** *The original test pressing and unused record label for* THE RADHA KRISHNA TEMPLE *LP along with the sheet music for their hit single "Govinda"; the opened front and back cover for the album autographed by artist/arranger Mukunda Goswami;* **SECOND ROW** SHANKAR FAMILY AND FRIENDS *autographed by Ravi Shankar and his corpulent percussionist Alla Rakha (Dark Horse Records 1974);* GODDESS OF FORTUNE, *a reissue of the original Apple Krishna album by the International Society for Krishna Consciousness (ISKCON); the soundtrack to Ravi Shankar's autobiographical film* RAGA, *autographed by sarod virtuoso Ali Akbar Khan, percussionist Alla Rakha and sitarist Shankar (Apple Records, 1971);* **BOTTOM ROW** LORD SITAR, *once thought to be a sneaky George Harrison solo album, this collection of favourite sixties tunes played on the sitar had nothing at all to do with the former Fab (Durcretet, Thompson, date unknown);* RAVI SHANKAR'S MUSIC FESTIVAL FROM INDIA *(Dark Horse Records 1976);* IN CONCERT *(Apple Records, 1972).*

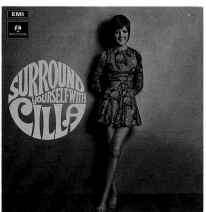
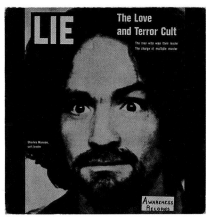
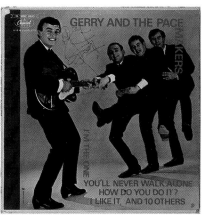
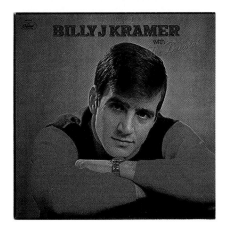
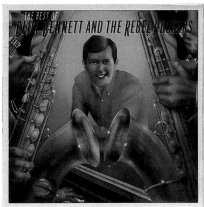
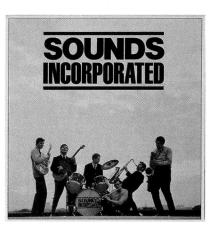

*Beatle friends and associates:* **TOP ROW** *Harry Nilsson,* PUSSY CATS *(RCA Records, 1974); Peter and Gordon's* I GO TO PIECES *(Capitol Records, 1965);* THE FOOL *(Mercury Records, 1969);* **SECOND ROW** *Cilla Black,* SURROUND YOURSELF WITH CILLA *(Parlophone Records, 1969); Charles Manson,* LIE. *The only relation between Charles Manson and the Beatles was in the convicted murderer's own troubled mind. But somehow his great love for the group and the popular notion that hidden messages in their music inspired him to order the murders of actress Sharon Tate and friends have convinced some of a connection (Awareness Records, 1970); Gerry and the Pacemakers,* I'M THE ONE! *autographed by Gerry Marsden (Capitol Records, 1964);* **BOTTOM ROW** *Billy J. Kramer,* THE BEST OF BILLY J. KRAMER *(Capitol Records, 1979); Cliff Bennett,* THE BEST OF CLIFF BENNETT AND THE REBEL ROUSERS *(EMI Records, date unknown); and Sounds Incorporated,* SOUNDS INCORPORATED *(See For Miles Records, 1983).*

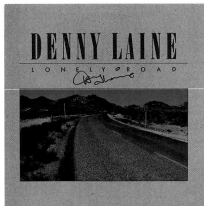

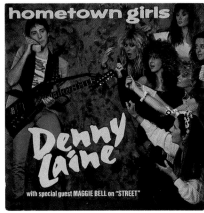

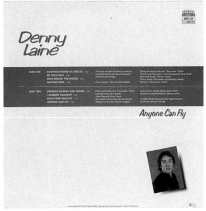

*Solo work by the multi-talented Denny Laine:* **TOP ROW** *Go Now (Global Records, 1980); Lonely Road (President Records, 1988); Ahh Laine! (Wizard Records, 1973);* **SECOND ROW** *Master Suite (Thunderbolt Records, 1988); Hometown Girls (President Records, 1985); a promotional twelve-inch single for Laine's classic "Go Now" (Rio Digital Records, 1988);* **BOTTOM ROW** *Wings On My Feet (President Records, 1987); Anyone Can Fly (Global Records, 1982); and Holly Days (EMI Records, 1977);* **OPPOSITE PAGE, TOP** *Denny Laine's autographed press photo and* **(BOTTOM RIGHT)** *personal calling card, while still a member of Wings;* **BOTTOM LEFT** *Promo pic issued by EMI.*

Denny Laine                    SCRATCH RECORDS    RCA

DENNY LAINE & PAUL McCARTNEY    EMI

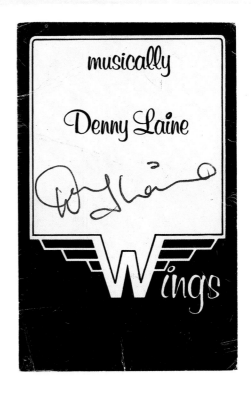

musically

Denny Laine

Wings

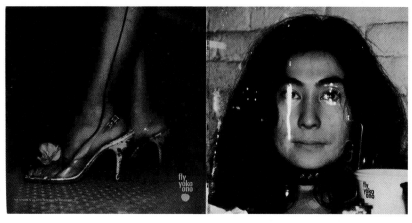

*Recorded works of Yoko Ono:* **TOP ROW** *SEASON OF GLASS, featuring the macabre image of the blood-stained glasses John Lennon wore the night he was murdered (Geffen Records, 1981); STARPEACE, released to coincide with Mrs Lennon's 1986 tour (Polygram Records, 1985); FEELING THE SPACE (Apple Records, 1973);* **SECOND ROW** *The open-front gatefold for Ono's FLY, cover photographs by John Lennon (Apple Records, 1971); IT'S ALRIGHT, autographed by the artist (Polygram Records, 1982);* **BOTTOM ROW** *The back cover to Yoko Ono's PLASTIC ONO BAND (Apple Records, 1970), and the front cover of APPROXIMATELY INFINITE UNIVERSE (Apple Records, 1972).*

**TOP ROW** *The back covers to Yoko Ono's* APPROXIMATELY INFINITE UNIVERSE *(Apple Records 1972) and* FEELING THE SPACE *(Apple Records, 1973);* **SECOND ROW** *The ghostly figure of John Lennon appears next to a flesh-and-blood Yoko and Sean on the back cover of Ono's* IT'S ALRIGHT *(Polygram Records, 1982); the free poster included in Yoko's two-record tribute to the art of noise,* FLY *(Apple Records, 1971).*

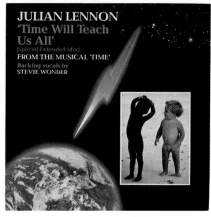

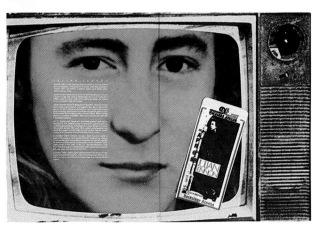

**OPPOSITE PAGE, LEFT** *An in-store graphic for Yoko's post-Lennon album,* IT'S ALRIGHT; **OPPOSITE PAGE, RIGHT** *A US poster to promote Julian Lennon's* THE SECRET VALUE OF DAYDREAMING *(1986);* **ABOVE** *Singles from Julian Lennon:* **TOP ROW** *"Too Late for Goodbyes" (Virgin Records, 1984); "Say You're Wrong" (Virgin Records, 1984); "This is My Day" (Charisma Records, 1986);* **SECOND ROW** *"Stick Around" (Charisma Records, 1986); "Time Will Teach Us All" (EMI Records, 1986); "Valotte" (Famous Charisma Records, 1984);* **BOTTOM ROW** *"Say You're Wrong" (Charisma Records, 1985) and "Want Your Body" (Charisma Records, 1986); the programme for Julian's 1986 tour and an all-access backstage pass; "Too Late For Goodbyes," (Atlantic Records, 1984) and "Now You're in Heaven" (Atlantic Records, 1989).*

TOP ROW *Julian Lennon's first albums,* THE SECRET VALUE OF DAYDREAMING *(Charisma Records, 1986) and* VALOTTE *autographed by the artist (Famous Charisma Records, 1984);* BELOW *The dramatic promotional poster for Julian Lennon's album* MR. JORDAN.

ABOVE *Beatle rip-off LPs:* TOP ROW THE CHIPMUNKS SING THE BEATLES *(Liberty Records, 1964); the Liverpools'* BEATLE MANIA! (IN THE USA) *(Quality Records, 1964); various artists'* BEATLESONGS!, *an interesting collection of Fab Four-related novelty tunes, sporting a disgraceful front cover illustration depicting John Lennon's assassin (extreme left) Mark David Chapman holding up a banner saying "We Love You Beatles". The cover was so distasteful that it was later withdrawn from sale and has hence become a valuable collector's item (Rhino Records, 1982);* SECOND ROW THE BEATLE BUDDIES, *an all-girl Beatle-style group promoted on the back cover as a product of "Synthetic Plastics Corporation, Newark, New Jersey." Perhaps this author's favourite Beatle-related lunacy (Diplomat Records, 1964); The Buggs'* THE BEETLE BEAT *(Coronet Records, 1964);* THE BROTHERS FOUR SING LENNON/MCCARTNEY *(Columbia, 1965);* BOTTOM ROW STARS ON LONG PLAY, *Dutch musician Jaap Eggermont's entertaining, disco-inspired tribute to the Fabs (Quality Records, 1981); the Koppykats'* THE BEATLES BEST *(Fontana Records, 1965); and* A TRIBUTE TO JOHN LENNON BY 101 STRINGS *(Alshire Records, 1980).*

 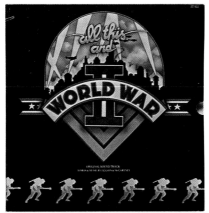 

 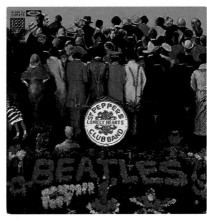 

*Only slightly more elevated musical scams:* **TOP ROW** *Graphics from the insane combination of Beatles cover tunes by well-known artists and the story of World War Two entitled* ALL THIS AND WORLD WAR TWO *(20th Century Records, 1976);* **SECOND ROW** THE BAROQUE BEATLES BOOK, *a synthesized rendition of the Fab Four's greatest hits (Elektra Records, date unknown); a clever electronic version of* SGT. PEPPER'S LONELY HEARTS CLUB BAND *by Japanese artist Jun Fukamachi (Toshiba Records, 1977);* THE BEATLES CONCERTO, *orchestrated versions of favourite Fab tunes (EMI Records, 1979);* **BOTTOM ROW** *Even Beatle producer George Martin got into the act viz his three Beatles-related offerings:* OFF THE BEATLE TRACK *(EMI Records, 1964);* GEORGE MARTIN INSTRUMENTALLY SALUTES THE BEATLE GIRLS *(United Artists Records, 1966);* HELP! *(United Artists Records, date unknown).*

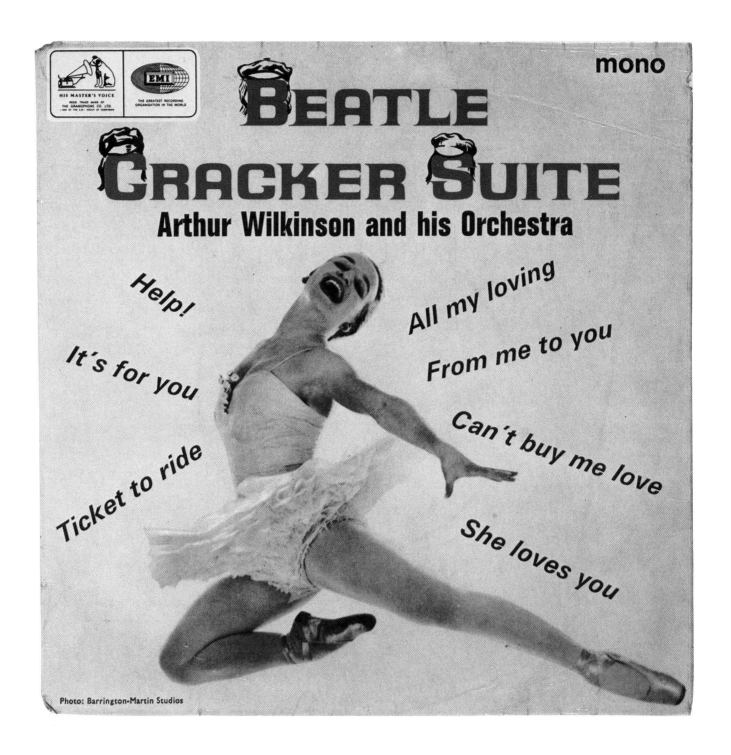

*The silly* BEATLE CRACKER SUITE *from those legendary giants of rock 'n' roll, Arthur Wilkinson and his Orchestra.*

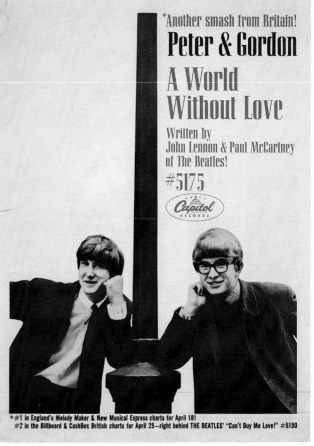

**TOP LEFT** *An autographed picture of Liverpool songstress Cilla Black, an old friend of the Beatles from their very early Cavern Club days;* **TOP RIGHT** *Then almost brother-in-law Paul McCartney and his pal John helping out Jane Asher's little brother Peter with his very own certified top ten hit;* **BELOW** *"The Big Three at the Cavern," a hard-to-find disc from those first fiery years of Merseymania (Decca Records, 1963).*

*"Baden-Powell's Foreskin," (collage over paint, 1989): the author's psychedelic vision of George Harrison as the mystical dark horse of the Beatles.*

**TOP** *John and Yoko join friends the Rolling Stones in their still-unreleased film*
ROCK AND ROLL CIRCUS, *December 12, 1968;* **BELOW** *Getting down at a session with the*
*Black Dyke Mills Band as Apple man Derek Taylor (left) looks on with folded arms, 1968;*
**OPPOSITE PAGE** *Taking it easy for world peace, 1969.*

OPPOSITE PAGE, ABOVE *Paul arrives at the London premiere of the animated film* YELLOW SUBMARINE, *July 1968;* OPPOSITE PAGE, BELOW *A dapper Ringo at the home of Beatle manager Brian Epstein, May 1967;* BELOW *John meets the press in Syracuse, New York, during Yoko's 1971 art show at the Everson Museum of Art;* BACKGROUND *St Peter's Parish Church in Woolton village where John and Paul first became acquainted in the mid-fifties.*

# JUBILEE
# MEMORABILIA

The peculiar pastime of collecting souvenirs of a bygone phenomenon like Beatlemania has over the years blossomed into a serious international preoccupation. Given the large sums of money regularly changing hands in the posh galleries of respectable auction houses like Sotheby's and Christie's, it can be a lucrative business. Still, despite such profit-centred pursuits, most of us out here slogging away to complete our ever-expanding collections do so for the love of it.

Interestingly, both John Lennon and Paul McCartney are known to have had their own private collections, regularly sending minions to auctions and conventions to buy up the very best Beatles goodies. John, it's been said, seemed to favour what he once termed "Beatle junk," silly things such as Beatle bobbing-head dolls, Beatle talcum powder, Beatle sneakers. Paul, on the other hand, seems to take the whole thing much more seriously, buying up not only original animation cells from the 1968 Beatles movie *Yellow Submarine*, but also going in for more meaty items such as old Beatle stage suits, musical instruments and even hand-written song lyrics

The Beatles' "new incarnation" as depicted on the cover of TIME, September 22, 1967. Illustration
by the noted British artist Gerald Scarfe, who later married ex-McCartney girlfriend Jane Asher
(© 1967 Time Warner Inc. Reprinted by permission).

*Original Beatle bubblegum cards, circa 1964.*

and design sketches for various Beatles albums.

In 1986, I spoke to Paul about the kind of things he had in his collection. "I've got odds and sods," he said. "I'm not a very thorough collector though because I haven't got all the records, for instance, which is daft. I really ought to have all of them. I've got some great little things, however, like my Hofner bass with the Beatles song list still taped onto it. I've got my Sgt. Pepper coat. I've got the first record we ever made, which is great."

Unlike Paul, who reportedly stores his collection in a warehouse on the outskirts of London, John used to enjoy his memorabilia in a more hands-on way. Famed singer and Lennon chum Harry Nilsson remembers an incident near the end of John's life, when a lucky Beatle fan happened to spot the composer walking around Manhattan sporting a large vintage 1964 lapel button stating, "I LOVE PAUL." After a few minutes of surreptitiously shadowing her idol, the anxious young woman finally summoned up the courage to approach him: "Excuse me, John, but why are you wearing a button that says, 'I LOVE PAUL?'" Without missing a beat, Lennon looked down at the girl through his famous gold-wire-rim glasses and declared, "Because I love Paul!" So much for the often-told tales of bitter jealousy and even hatred between the two former partners.

Of the many categories of bona fide memorabilia, perhaps the two most desirable are the original mass-produced products put out during the heyday of worldwide Beatlemania in 1964 and 1965 and the coveted one-of-a-kind personal items touched by the Beatles themselves. Of all Beatle-related ephemera, these are by far the most costly, with price tags ranging in the thousands for the more personalized pieces.

Of the mass-produced type, the sky is the limit as a whole array of bizarre souvenirs were marketed to the Beatle-crazed youth of Great Britain, America and beyond. For example, one Chicago firm even flogged canned

"Beatles' Breath." Following a Kansas City concert, an enterprising pair paid $1,000 for several bed sheets upon which the boys reportedly had slept, then cut the sheets into 150,000 one-inch pieces and offered the cotton squares to the youth of the world for a mere $10 each.

A number of licencing deals were also put together under the auspices of New York businessman Nicky Byrne for Seltaeb Limited (Beatles spelled backward), which in turn had a deal with NEMS Enterprises in London overseen by Beatles' manager Brian Epstein. A total of 234 products were listed with the company at the time of Epstein's death in 1967, including such oddities as Beatles egg cups, airbeds, cutlery, ladies' fancy garters with lockets, coat hangers, a Beatles bingo game, ladies' briefs, wallpaper, plastic disposable drinking cups and even Beatles toenail clippers. Among the more bizarre proposals for which licences were thankfully never granted was for a Beatles sanitary napkin emblazoned with the likeness of each of the Fabs.

My personal involvement in all things Beatle began in earnest back in the summer of 1968 when I first saw John and Yoko's *Two Virgins*. It was owned by a friend whom I eventually talked out of his prized mint copy. Every once in awhile, I would take the record out of my closet just to look at it and to think, "Wow, this is neat. Weird . . . but neat." The next hard-to-find record I got my hands on was George Harrison's Moog synthesizer experiment *Electronic Sound*. After listening to it a couple of times, I decided that no music was "supposed" to sound like that. After a few days I took it right back to the same neighborhood Rexall drugstore where I had bought it and demanded my money back.

"There's something wrong with this record, man," I said to the slightly hipper-than-average looking guy behind the counter. "A lot of squawking noises and things is there?" he asked. "Yeah," I replied. "And static too. Lots of it." "It's called avant-garde." Boy did I feel stupid. A few weeks later while attending my first real rock concert (Steppenwolf), I met a guy I knew from school who sold me a tab of Strawberry Barrel LSD for three bucks and I took my first mind-conditioning trip. After that, *Electronic Sound* and *Two Virgins* became my very favourite records. I used to sit in my little bedroom and listen to them both virtually non-stop for days. I guess I had become avant-garde too.

*An early shot of the Beatles given out to members of the Beatle Fan Club, complete with printed autographs.*

*A young John Lennon poses with his infant sister Julia in this rare photo, autographed by Julia.*

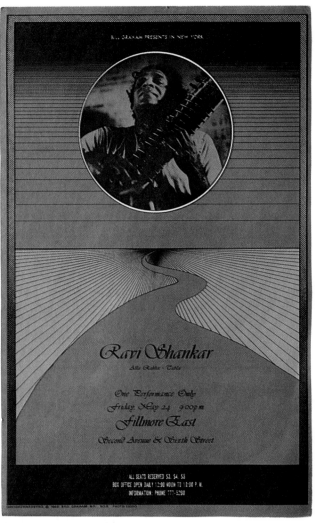

**Paul McCartney**
Serie P - Printed in Holland No. 12

**John Lennon**
Serie P - Printed in Holland No. 5

TOP LEFT *A colourful lobby card used to promote the Beatles' animated psychedelic adventure* YELLOW SUBMARINE; TOP RIGHT *Ravi Shankar in performance at the famous Fillmore East, May 24, 1968;* BOTTOM *Two hard-to-find trading cards printed in Holland in the mid-seventies.*

Great to have you with us

George Harrison

Ringo Starr

Paul McCartney

John Lennon

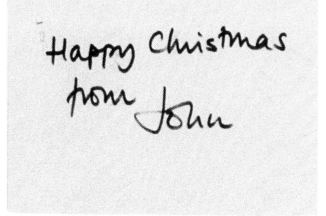

OPPOSITE PAGE *An autographed original from the Fab Four, circa 1965;* ABOVE, TOP LEFT *Almost 30 years after the Beatles first burst upon the scene, their faithful fans still gather regularly around the globe. This poster advertises one such event;* TOP RIGHT WINGS GREATEST *(Capitol Records, 1978) autographed for the author by Paul and Linda McCartney and Wings star Denny Laine, and* (BELOW) *a Christmas greeting from John Lennon to a family friend;* BOTTOM *A valuable in-store flyer for Harrison's "Dark Horse," the single from 1974.*

*A signed picture of George, recently discovered in the files of a popular American celebrity magazine.*

*Two pages from the delightful pop-up book THE BEATLES STORY by Rob Burt and Michael Wells (Orbis Books, London, 1985). One spread* **(BOTTOM)** *shows the Beatles high on LSD, love and light during their psychedelic* SGT. PEPPER *period. The other* **(TOP)** *portrays the group playing from the rooftops of London during their final days together. Note Phil Spector, Linda Eastman and Allen Klein, among others, in the windows.*

*Beatle-related movie cards:* **TOP ROW** *A rare lobby card from* THE FAMILY WAY *film, score by Paul McCartney; Ringo Starr romances Ewa Aulin in the Terry Southern film adaptation of* CANDY, *1969;* **SECOND AND BOTTOM ROWS** *Four views from* A HARD DAY'S NIGHT, *1964.*

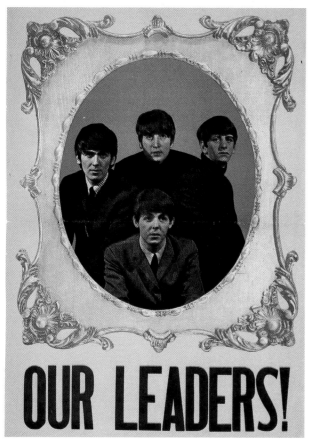

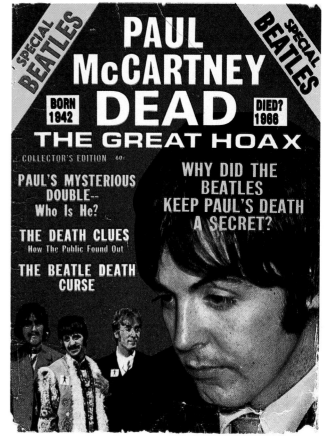

*Vintage Beatles silliness from the mid-sixties:* **BOTTOM RIGHT** *Did Paul McCartney really die in a terrible 1966 auto crash? This so-called collector's edition magazine* THE GREAT HOAX *seems to think so.*

*To Arjuna best wishes – George Harrison*

**GEORGE HARRISON**

®LOKA PRODUCTIONS, S.A.
Printed in U.S.A.

*Harrison sends greetings to a fan.*

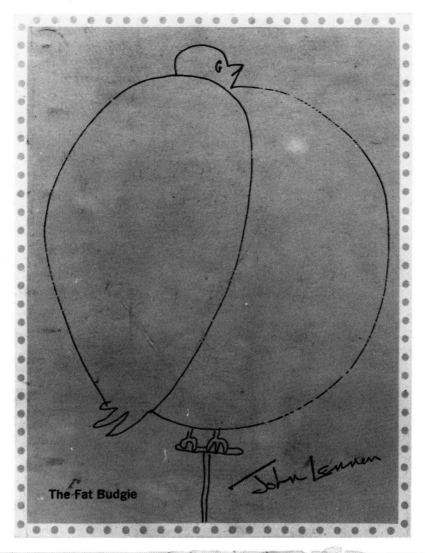

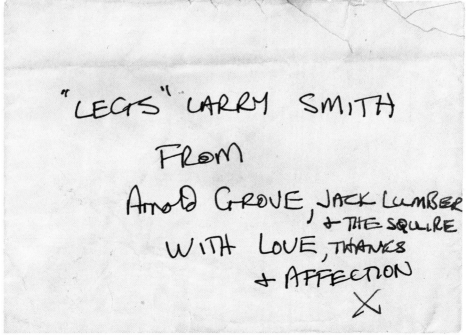

TOP *This obscure Fat Budgie greeting card from 1965 was designed and illustrated by John Lennon;* BOTTOM *George pens a note to an old friend using the aliases Arnold Grove, Jack Lumber and The Squire.*

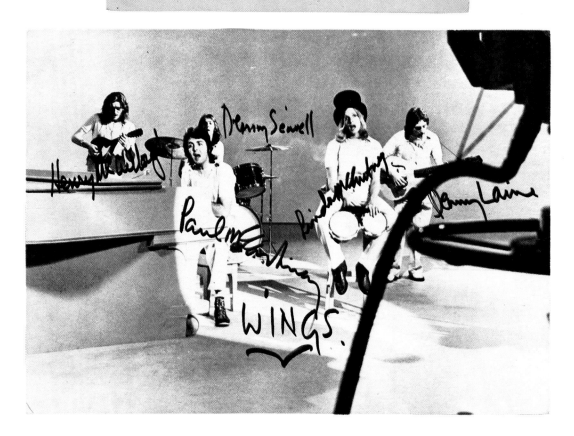

TOP *The striking original sheet music to the Beatles' optimistic* SGT. PEPPER *piece "Getting Better";*
BOTTOM *An autographed picture of Wings in its first configuration, 1972.*

**TOP ROW** *An impossible-to-find original John and Yoko Apple postcard based on a photograph taken of the couple during their 1969 honeymoon in Paris; a one-of-a-kind poster from Brian Epstein's short-lived Saville Theatre. Note the appearance on the bill of future Wings collaborator Denny Laine;* **BOTTOM ROW** *A rare Beatle Fan Club poster from 1970 photographed at Tittenhurst Park, 1969.*

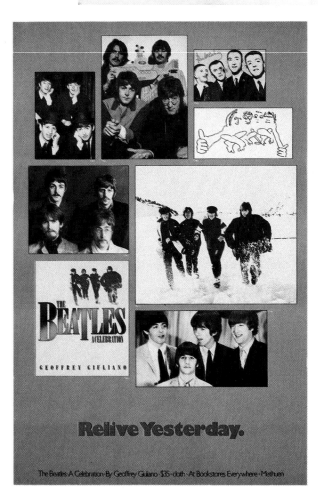

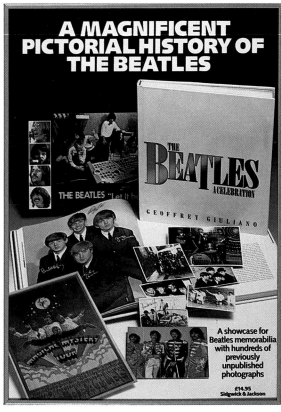

TOP *The logo of the Beatle Fan Club shortly after it moved from Liverpool to London;* BOTTOM ROW
*Two limited-edition posters promoting the author's first book* THE BEATLES: A CELEBRATION: LEFT
*The Canadian edition from Methuen Publications, Toronto, 1986;* RIGHT *British publisher
Sidgwick & Jackson's graphic from the same year.*

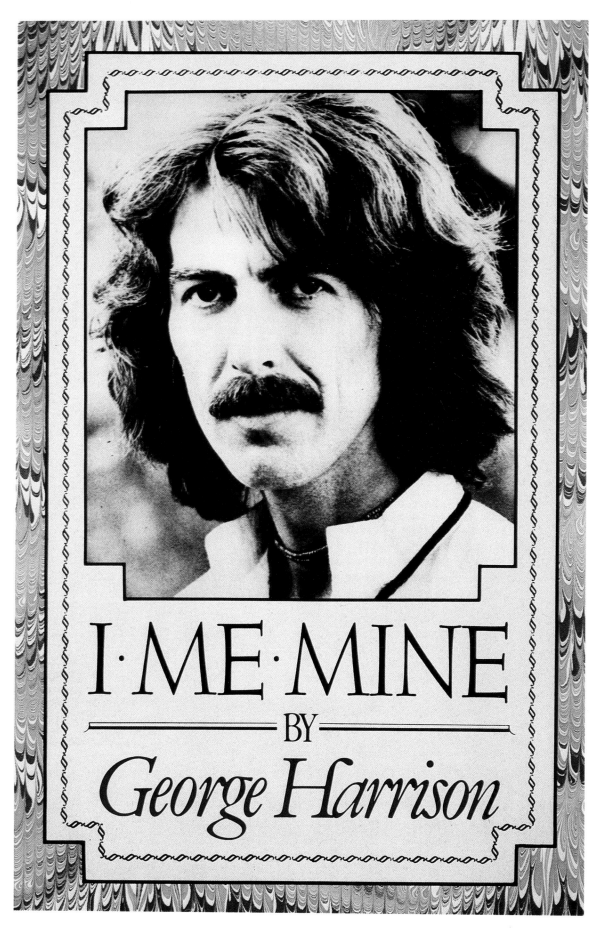

*A limited-run poster for George Harrison's autobiographical collection of song lyrics, photographs and interviews, I ME MINE (Genesis Publications, 1980).*

TOP ROW *Two posters advertising Wings' early tours;* BOTTOM *A mid-seventies fold-out poster included as part of a British newsstand publication on Paul McCartney and Wings;* OPPOSITE PAGE *An elaborate Wings press kit from the mid-seventies.*

Jimmy McC...

WINGS

...DA and PAUL McCART...

As a point of purchase promotional tactic, record companies often printed up a number of reproductions of an album's front cover. These "slicks" are then plastered around retail outlets to help increase awareness of their product. **TOP ROW** Slicks for Wings' BACK TO THE EGG; George's GEORGE HARRISON; and the Beatles' REEL MUSIC; **BOTTOM** A poster for the epic Ringo Starr spaghetti western BLIND MAN (1971); **OPPOSITE PAGE** The selling of the Beatles and friends. Original press kits designed to garner yet more publicity for those already in the upper echelons of rock 'n' roll.

CERTIFIED COPY OF AN ENTRY OF BIRTH

GIVEN AT THE GENERAL REGISTER OFFICE,
SOMERSET HOUSE, LONDON.

Application Number ___663300___

| No. | When and where born | Name, if any | Sex | Name, and surname of father | Name, surname, and maiden surname of mother | Occupation of father | Signature, description and residence of informant | When registered | Signature of registrar | Name entered after registration |
|---|---|---|---|---|---|---|---|---|---|---|
| 453 | Ninth October 1940 Liverpool Maternity Hospital u.d. | John Winston | Boy | Alfred Lennon | Julia Lennon formerly Stanley | Steward (Steamship) 9 Newcastle Road Liverpool 15 u.d. | A. Lennon Father 9 Newcastle Road Liverpool 15 | Eleventh November 1940 | J.R. Kirkwood Registrar | |

REGISTRATION DISTRICT _Liverpool South_

1940. BIRTH in the Sub-district of _Abercromby_ in the _County Borough of Liverpool_

CERTIFIED to be a true copy of an entry in the certified copy of a Register of Births in the District above mentioned.
Given at the GENERAL REGISTER OFFICE, SOMERSET HOUSE, LONDON, under the Seal of the said Office, the 19th day of November 1968

BC 655765

CERTIFIED COPY OF AN ENTRY OF BIRTH

GIVEN AT THE GENERAL REGISTER OFFICE,
SOMERSET HOUSE, LONDON.

Application Number ___663299___

| No. | When and where born | Name, if any | Sex | Name, and surname of father | Name, surname, and maiden surname of mother | Occupation of father | Signature, description and residence of informant | When registered | Signature of registrar | Name entered after registration |
|---|---|---|---|---|---|---|---|---|---|---|
| 226 | Seventh July 1940 9 Madryn Street u.d. | Richard | Boy | Richard Starkey | Elsie Starkey formerly Gleave | Confectioner (Cake maker) | E. Starkey Mother 9 Madryn Street Liverpool 8 | Twenty first July 1940 | M.J. Nichols Registrar | — |

REGISTRATION DISTRICT _Liverpool South_

1940. BIRTH in the Sub-district of _Toxteth Park_ in the _County Borough of Liverpool_

CERTIFIED to be a true copy of an entry in the certified copy of a Register of Births in the District above mentioned.
Given at the GENERAL REGISTER OFFICE, SOMERSET HOUSE, LONDON, under the Seal of the said Office, the 19th day of November 1968

BC 655797

TOP ROWS *Facsimiles of the Beatles' birth certificates published in England during the late sixties;* BOTTOM *Rare original pieces from the photographic assemblage used in the famous backdrop of* SGT. PEPPER: (LEFT) *Richard Lindner and actor W.C. Fields,* (RIGHT) *A woman modelled after Charles Dana Gibson's famous Gibson Girl;* OPPOSITE PAGE *Beatles and company original concert programmes from around the world.*

TOP *Since the singer's tragic death in December 1980, the memory of John Lennon has been faithfully preserved by his second wife Yoko Ono. In 1988, a Warner Brothers documentary* IMAGINE *on the former Beatle was released to critical acclaim. This is the poster for the film;* BOTTOM *Valued at more than $15,000, this one-of-a-kind handmade tapestry depicting John and Yoko was originally intended as part of a limited-edition based on two of the late Beatle's drawings. This particular colour configuration was ultimately scrapped by Ono as being "too depressing." As a result, this prototype is now highly prized.*

*A simple yet effective poster to mark the release of music from the 1988 movie documentary* IMAGINE.

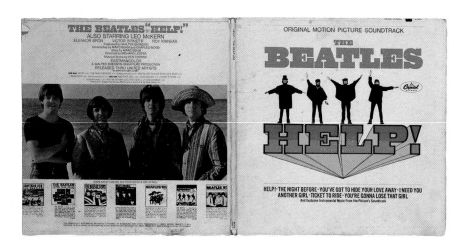

*Marketing the Beatles' second movie* HELP! *Included in this assemblage of memorabilia relating to the high-energy feature are the hardbound book, various press photos, the album cover, a deluxe press kit and even a VIP pass for one of the several American premieres.*

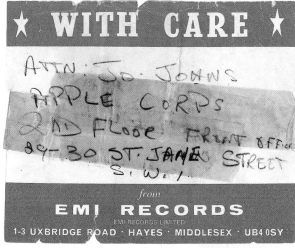

**TOP** *Probably the single rarest piece of original sixties Beatles memorabilia in existence today, a handcrafted throw rug from England depicting four boyish Beatles. Interestingly, this particular piece once belonged to George Harrison's son Dhani, but is now in the collection of the author;* **BOTTOM LEFT** *An EMI Records mailing label personally addressed by John Lennon;* **BOTTOM RIGHT** *After John Lennon's murder, his label Geffen Records destroyed all promotional materials produced for the album* DOUBLE FANTASY *for fear of being seen as cashing in on the singer's tragic death. Fortunately for hardcore fans a few highly prized items from John and Yoko's prophetic swan song still survive today. Among them, this "browser box" designed to display the single "(Just Like) Starting Over" is perhaps one of the most desirable.*

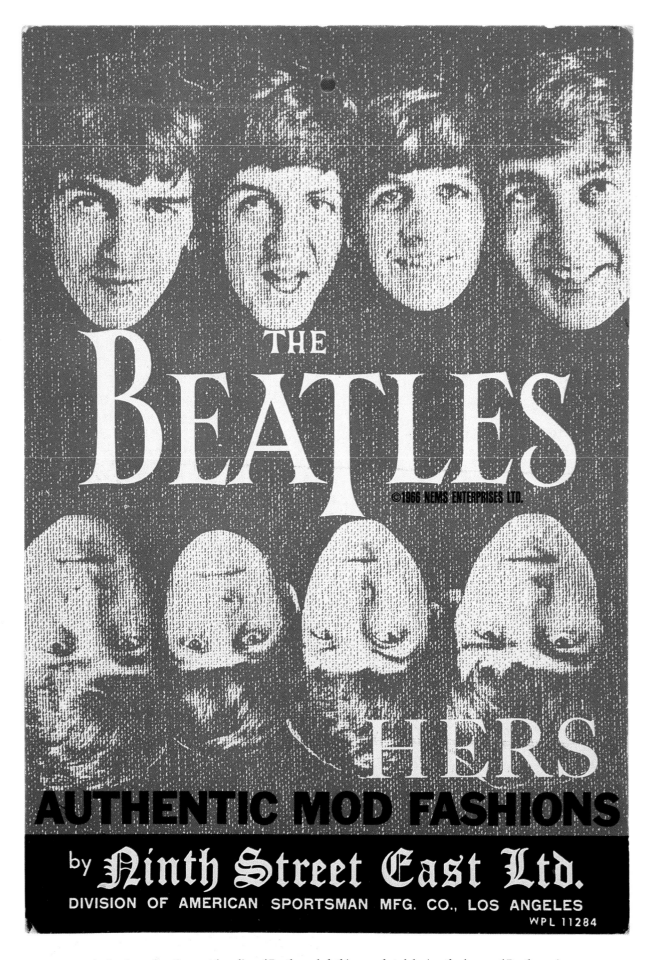

*An in-store advertisement for a line of Beatle mod clothing marketed during the frenzy of Beatlemania.*

*A pot-pourri of ads for Beatle products that
proliferated during the mid-sixties.*

**TOP** *An original pencil character sketch for the Beatles' cartoon dream* YELLOW SUBMARINE;
**BOTTOM** *At first the city fathers of Liverpool were slow to celebrate the achievements of their famous native sons. However, after repeated outcries from fans, they finally commissioned this surprisingly impressive media kit which was sent to journalists and fans in the early seventies.*

TOP *The poster for "This is not Here," a 1971 conceptual art exhibition by Yoko Ono, with "guest artist" John Lennon, at the Everson Museum of Art, Syracuse, New York;* BOTTOM *A 1981 poster promoting the superlative 30-hour radio documentary on the group, produced by Sonic Workshop, Toronto, Canada.*

**TOP ROW** *Ringo and wife Barbara Bach, like all the Beatles, occasionally send out autographs to a few select fans. These two autographs were received in the late eighties, following the couple's move from their Tittenhurst Park estate;* **BOTTOM** *Paul's rough sketch for the album cover of* LONDON TOWN.

"Second-generation" Beatle memorabilia, including a potentially collectible Traveling Wilbury's electric guitar purchased for the author's son by former Wings' co-commander Denny Laine. Also pictured, a limited-edition commemorative John Lennon plate flanked by an assortment of already valuable vintage collectibles, including a Beatle change purse, a 1962 Cavern Club membership card and a YELLOW SUBMARINE picture puzzle.

TOP *John and Yoko deeply in love during a quiet moment at their famous Bed-In For Peace in Amsterdam, 1969;* BOTTOM *Ringo and Maureen after they first got married.*

TOP *Paul, Linda and Stella McCartney arriving at Heathrow Airport, England, September 1976;*
BOTTOM *George and Pattie on their wedding day.*

TOP *Ringo, George and company fly off to the South of France from London to attend the Cannes Film Festival, May 1972;* BOTTOM *Leaving a local London court following a hearing on marijuana charges stemming from a 1968 raid on their Montague Square flat.*

# INDEX

# ACKNOWLEDGEMENTS

The author gratefully acknowledges the kind and invaluable assistance of the following in the production of this work: Abbey Road Studios; James Adams; AIR Studios (London); Apple Corp Ltd; The BBC; Meher Baba; Ginger Baker; Barrymore Barlow; Avie Bennett; Pete Best; Deborah Lyn Black; Raymond and Sadie Black; Fred and Chris Brown; Larry Brown; Peter Buck; Brant and Maria Cowie; Bo Diddley; Donovan; Michael Downey; Dragon's World Ltd; Steve Ebby; Glen Ellis; Dr. Bradden Fitz-Gerald; Robert John Gallo; Robert Noel Giuliano; Robin Scott Giuliano; Sesa, Devin, Avalon and India; "Whispering" Bob Harris; Bob "The Bear" Hite; Mary Hopkin; Ian Hundley; William Hushion; ISKCOW; Neil Innes; Joe Jelly; Carla Johnson; Jimmy Kanaris; Susan Muirsmith Kent; Ben E. King; Coretta Scott King; Marvin Kirshman; Jo Jo Laine; Allan Lang; Leif Leavesley; Tanya Long; Andrew Lownie; Trish Lyon; The MGA Agency; MPL Communications; His Divine Grace Bhakti Hirday Magalniloy Maharaj; Gerry Marsden; Mike and Rowena McCartney; The Merseyside Tourist Board; Methuen Publications; The Nolan/Lehr Group; Frank Poole; Michael Powers; Jerry Powers; His Divine Grace A. C. Bhaktividanta Swami Prabhupada; Jane Price and Summer; Keith Reinhard; Charles F. Rosenay !!!; Pippa Rubinstein; Roger Ruskin Spear; Dimo Safari; Skyboot Productions Ltd; "Legs" Larry Smith; Something Fishy Productions Ltd; Spiritual Realization Institute (SRI); Sarah Silberstein Swartz; Jim Swick; John Sylvano; Dennis P. Toll; Anthony Violanti; Ernie Williams; "Blind Owl" Wilson; Bob Wooler; Dr. Ronald Zuker.

## Credits

Specific credits are found throughout this book. Every effort has been made to obtain permission for the use of illustrations reproduced wherever possible. We apologize for any unintentional errors, omissions or infringements on copyright. These will be corrected in future editions: Abbey Road/EMI Studios; Aidart; Alshire Records; Americom Corp.; Apple Records; Atco Records; Atlantic Records; Audifon Records; Backstage Records; Bag Records; Barking Moose Records; Beetle Records; Bellaphone Records; Blackbird Records; Boardwalk Records; Breakaway Records; Capitol Records; Charisma Records; Circut Records; Collectable Record Corp.; Collectables Records; Contra Band Records; Core Records; Coronet Records; Cotillion Records; Custom Recording; Dakota Records; Dark Horse Records; Decca Records; Deccagone Records; Democratic Records; De Weintraub Records; Diplomat Records; DJM Records; Durcretet, Thompson; E.H.M.V. Records; Elektra Records; EMI Records; Epic Records; Erika Records; EVA Records; Famous Charisma Records; Fan Records; Fontana Records; Geffen Records; Global Records; Gnat Records; Handmade Records; Hocus Pocus Records; Imperial Records; Island Records; Jet Records; Joker Records; Denny Laine Music; Liberty Records; Lingasong Records; Loka Records; Love & Peace Records; MCA Records; Melodiya Records; Mercury Records; Midwest Records; Moonchild Records; Moriphon Records; Music for Pleasure; NEMS Records; New Sound Records; Object Enterprises; Odeon Records; Orange Records; Overseas Records; Parlophone Records; Pod Records; Polydor Records; Polygram Records; President Records; PRC Recording Co.; Pye Studio; Quality Records; Raven Records; RCA Records; Rhino Records; Ring O' Records; Rio Digital Records; Ruthless Rymes Records; Sandwich Records; Savage Records; Scratch Records; See for Miles Records; Silhouette Records; Startline Records; Swan Records; Thunderbolt Records; Toshiba Records; 20th Century Records; UFO Records; Underside Records; United Artists; Vee Jay Records; Virgin Records; Warner Bros Records; Warwick Records; WEA Records; Wibble Records; Wilbury Records; Wizard Records; Wizardo Records; Zapple Records.

## Photograph Credits

PUBLIC DOMAIN 3 (early publicity handout), 6, 219, 222 (publicity photographs); © SKYBOOT PRODUCTION LTD 8, 32/33 [background], 70/71 [background], 94/95 [background], 120/121 [background], 167 [background], 186/187 [background], 214/215 [background], 238 [bottom row]; COURTESY PINK SHOES CAFE 28, 29, 30, 31, 32, 33, 68, 69 [bottom], 70, 71, 92, 93, 94, 95, 118 [top], 119, 120, 121, 135 [bottom], 138 [top], 140, 160 [bottom], 164 [bottom], 165, 166, 167 [top], 182 [bottom left], 184 [top], 185, 186, 187, 212, 213, 214, 215, 224, 248 [top row], 250, 251, 252; © DIMO SAFARI 62; © CHRIS WALTER 69 [top]; COURTESY COLUMBIA RECORDS 118 [bottom] (publicity photograph); COURTESY APPLE RECORDS (publicity photographs) 138 [bottom], 181 [bottom], 182 [except bottom left], 183; COURTESY DARK HORSE RECORDS (publicity photographs) 139, 141, 228; COURTESY EMI RECORDS (publicity photographs) 164 [top], 230 [bottom]; COURTESY YORKSHIRE TELEVISION 167 [bottom]; COURTESY MELODY MAKER 184 [bottom]; COURTESY NEIL INNES 191 [top]; COURTESY THE DIXON AGENCY (publicity photograph) 195 [top]; COURTESY MY PERNA PRODUCTIONS LTD 220.

Beatles memorabilia COURTESY THE GIULIANO COLLECTION.

Special thanks to Peter Max for his enthusiasm and unshakeable belief in this project, Brandon Stickney for the swell research and Toni Hafkenscheid for his fabulous photographs of the memorabilia included within.

This book is dedicated to Brenda Giuliano for her love, encouragement, loyalty and faith unending.